Advertising BRITISH CARS *of the* 50s

HEON STEVENSON

Foulis

Haynes
®

A **Foulis** Motoring Book

First published 1991

© Heon Stevenson 1991

Published by:
Haynes Publishing Group
Sparkford, Nr Yeovil
Somerset BA22 7JJ, England

Haynes Publications Inc
861 Lawrence Drive, Newbury Park,
California 91320, USA

**British Library Cataloguing in Publication
Data**

A catalogue record for this book is available
from the British Library

ISBN 0 85429 898 3

Library of Congress Catalog card number
91–73000

Editor: Rod Grainger
Design and layout: Mike King
Typeset in Triumvirate Medium 9/10 pt.
Printed in England by J. H. Haynes & Co. Ltd.

Contents

Foreword

The postwar car advertisement, as an object of interest in its own right, has been largely overlooked. Whilst much has been written about the cars of the 1950s, the advertisements which persuaded the public to purchase those automobiles have not, for the most part, been studied in detail. This book is an attempt to redress the balance.

I should say at the outset that what follows is in no sense intended as a history of the postwar British car under another name, but rather a study of the advertising themes of the period, though as a collection, these advertisements do represent a cross-section of the automobiles available during the fifties.

These advertisements have in abundance that ill-defined but powerful quality, "period charm". Much that is mediocre can be canonized by the mere whisper of that phrase, and I leave it to the reader to judge which are the good, and which are the less good of the advertisements which follow, if it matters at all.

From the perspective of the 1990s, it is interesting to see what themes have endured, and what, on the other hand, is not reflected in the modern climate. There are some surprising similarities between certain ancient and modern advertisements, while at the same time, some publicity material is very much of its own era, and is unlikely to be echoed by later work.

Most of the advertisements shown in this book have not been taken from motoring papers of the fifties, but from magazines which had little to do with automobiles. The advertisements would therefore have been aimed not only at the enthusiast, but at the general reader with no particular interest in the motorcar as a technical object. A corollary of this non-specialized emphasis is that many of the advertisements shown in this book were not printed in the motoring magazines of the day in the same form, if at all. Thus I hope that what follows will augment, rather than duplicate what the enthusiast is able to acquire through other, specialist, channels. I hope also that these advertisements will interest not only the automobile enthusiast, but also the reader with a general interest in what is, without doubt, a fascinating period in the development of British consumerism.

Acknowledgements

A book such as this relies upon the availability of historical material, and I am therefore most grateful to the following for allowing reproduction of their advertisements: Rover Cars (Austin, MG, Morris, Riley, Rover, Standard-Triumph, Wolseley), Land-Rover (Land-Rover), Ford Motor Co. Ltd. (Ford), the Peugeot Talbot Motor Co. Ltd. (Hillman, Humber, Singer, Sunbeam), the Reliant Group Plc (Bond), Vauxhall Motors Ltd. (Vauxhall), Jaguar Cars Ltd. (Jaguar, Daimler, Lanchester), Goodyear GB Ltd. (Vauxhall PA Cresta/Goodyear) and to Bob Murray, editor of *Autocar & Motor* (Bond, Berkeley, Triumph TR3).

*I*ntroduction

"In Greek mythology, Orion was a mighty hunter; in the constellations, he remains immortalized amongst the stars." Would this pronouncement persuade you to buy the latest version of an unattractive car? The modern reader of this 1955 advertisement for the Singer Hunter may well wonder. Ironically, and unbeknown to the advertisement's original audience, the car would cease production a year later, having sold less than five thousand examples. With it went the maker, too, as in 1956 Singer was taken over by the Rootes Group, and the name survived only on glorified Hillmans.

In contrast to the laboured and self-conscious eulogizing which plagued the last days of the Hunter, Bentley and Jaguar could afford to be more aloof. An evocative series of advertisements for the Bentley depicted the latest model against an industrial backdrop, where the owner of the factory and of the Bentley is seen with another businessman, or possibly an accountant, discussing a decision, while in the foreground is seen the "plant", with work being carried out within. The Bentley is portrayed as a natural accoutrement to shrewd and careful business planning – though what the workers thought of the car is not recorded! It was not necessary to lower the tone to a discussion of the car's mechanical merits, which were assumed.

A less prestigious car whose advertising has suffered at the hands of posterity is the Wolseley 6/90, which was advertised by means of an oily pastiche of middle-class manners which today amuses. A 6/90 allegedly conferred the doubtful virtue of "*esprit de car*" to augment the owner's "pride of self" which would no doubt fail dismally if deprived of such props as the 1956 saloon. In another piece, "Giles" and "Charles" debate the relative merits of the 6/90 and the smaller 4/44, Giles proclaiming that his colleague's 4/44 has "wonderful performance for a 1¼ litre" while Charles admits to "hankering" after the extra performance of the larger car. They agree – and surely the copywriter must here have had tongue firmly in cheek – that the cars have "a kind of quiet distinction which is difficult to explain, but which conveys a lot to one's friends". It would be churlish to ask what exactly might be conveyed, other than relative wealth. The cars were cheap enough to be afforded by those unable to buy a genuinely exclusive car, but who would not be seen dead in a Vauxhall. Other advertisements of the genre parodied fashionable phrases – "*noblesse oblige*" was one – and emphasised the cars' supposed discretion. Both cars sold moderately well, and later advertisements were less neurotic.

These few examples illustrate the variety of approaches adopted by copywriters during the early part of the fifties. Ford and Austin emphasised solid virtues – the latter augmented by the worthy pipe-smoker, and with "Austin of England" badges to inject a note of jingoism into the copy, as well as that respectability of which the pipe was a sure sign. A less down to earth approach was favoured for the glamour models – Ford's Zodiac, and the Austin-Healey sports cars to name but two. Indeed, by the mid-fifties, cars were assumed to work well and lost sales rapidly if they did not. Not only was the home market becoming more critical; under harsh conditions abroad even quality cars had been found wanting, as wood-framed bodies supported by stiff suspensions rapidly wore out.

The Jowett Javelin was an unfortunate case of a good design, potentially very rugged, which was let down by under-development. In later advertisements for the car, what were trumpeted as "modifications resulting from five years of successful international competition work and strenuous overseas use" were vitally necessary for a car which, by popular repute, had enjoyed five years of breakdowns induced, *inter alia*, by engine flooding and gasket failure, run bearings and premature rusting, as stockpiled bodies started to corrode even before dispatch to owners. In fact, the Javelin was one of the most inspired cars of the early postwar period, with excellent handling, performance, interior space and build quality. This was not enough to persuade the buyers, however, and for a short while the Javelin was one of the few cars for which there was not a substantial waiting-list in Britain.

It is interesting to see how sales performance affected copy, and in retrospect the signs of good or poor sales can often be detected. A Javelin advertisement of 1953 was headed "Ever actually driven a Javelin yourself?", which suggested to the cynic that the early version's reputation for temperament when abused had masked the good name it enjoyed amongst those who understood it.

Clever advertisers were not those who indulged in wishful thinking as to the type of person who would buy the car – rather the actual market (which hopefully would also be the target market) was wooed with appropriately contrived phrases and motifs. Occasionally the car would be so slow-selling or old-fashioned that such tactics were not worthwhile. The copywriters for the unsuccessful Singer Hunter were clearly scraping the barrel in the advertisement quoted above, deserting Wolseley's smug innuendo for a wholly unsolicited frolic into obscure classical allusion, and inclusion of reference to independent front wheel suspension as late as 1955 clearly indicated desperation.

It was always useful to have some new feature to crow about – which, for the most part, Singer were denied – and Ford and Vauxhall policies of continuous improvement allowed modifications to be gleefully announced quite frequently. Moreover, it always helped if the potential buyer could see the cars roaring past by the dozen, or could get a lift to work in one, or in some other way could be convinced independently of a particular car's merit. If the car was unfamiliar, the maker started with a disadvantage, unless the product had a prodigious reputation.

In the case of the specialist models, the enthusiast could be relied upon to approach his or her choice of car with a certain amount of care and reason. For the family car buyer, to whom the machine was primarily an alternative to buses and trains, there was no real incentive to opt for something unusual, which had to be driven miles for a service, and with which mechanics would be unfamiliar. Here, Ford in particular won hands down, and the mention of "Ford service too" in advertisements was confidently made. "Make-sure" service schedules were useful as a means of quickly correcting any faults which did develop during the first few thousand miles of use, and replacement engines were available cheaply for high-mileage users. In short, the Ford service system was well co-ordinated, and in many respects was a benchmark which gathered as many sales as reams of elaborate copy may have done.

The increasing sophistication of the car buyer, and the consequent spread of a willingness to criticise inferior products have affected the style of the postwar motorcar advertisement. Earlier advertisements did not need to be too technical, as competition was not overly intense. Foreign cars in particular were imported in tiny numbers until the sixties, in spite of the use in competition of Borgwards and some Volvos. Moreover, the shortage of cars on the home market until 1955/56 did not breed fussiness in a population largely confined to elderly pre-war wrecks, exhumed from wartime slumber and deterioration. But this situation was to change, and the public became more critical. Furthermore, an increasing section of that public was not mechanically minded; the car had to work, and was pilloried if it did not.

Towards the late fifties, a pretty picture and a slogan, perhaps accompanied by a vague testimonial from a mythical owner, were no longer enough. Blocks of type beside pseudo-technical illustrations showed that the makers were trying a little harder. Not only did the car work, but it worked better because . . . All this gave buyers the impression that they were "in on the act", and therefore that their choice was a knowledgeable one. The customer could then be praised for good judgement. Wolseley stated that the choice of their car was a wise one, and other makers from time to time substituted "clever", "sophisticated", "intelligent" and so on, as appropriate.

On the other hand, image and glamour became pre-eminent as selling factors as the fifties ended and the sixties began. Daimler lost exclusive Royal patronage and so were unable to count on continued sales to old-fashioned snobs; the cars were increasingly marketed on their own merits, rather than with reference to time-honoured tradition, or, indeed, to time-honoured features like preselector gears. Ballerinas gave way to brake specifications and to claims of engineering excellence and, therefore, intrinsic prestige. Nevertheless, if a car was not pre-eminent by purely utilitarian criteria, a sophisticated image might disguise its inadequacies and persuade the would-be sophisticate that such priorities were not really the *raison d'être* of the car. Particular weaknesses of otherwise good cars could be subsumed beneath a general aura of excellence, as in the case of the Rolls-Royce Silver Cloud, which, depending on one's point of view, either encouraged or required a dignified style of driving, and whose auxiliary ashtrays, in wood-effect brown bakelite, looked like those of an earlier Vauxhall Wyvern. S. C. H. Davis put the point tactfully, preferring "all the smaller details to be essentially Rolls-Royce, so that owners of other cars would not notice similarities".

By the late fifties, more people could afford cars, and some of them could afford second cars for their wives. The rôle of the woman in car choice gradually changed, though that change would be most marked in the sixties. At the beginning of our period, the woman driver was relatively rare, and the woman who chose and owned her car independently of male influence rarer still. Many women could drive, especially as thousands had learnt both driving and maintenance skills on heavy vehicles during the war. There were also several female rally drivers of top rank. But no amount of hard achievement could persuade the copywriters that women were, as a matter of course, safe and competent behind the wheel, let alone that they understood how a car worked. There were exceptions. In 1953, Ford showed a woman at the wheel of a Consul, clearly indicating that she chose the car, used it herself, and drove it on business and not merely for the occasional trip to the shops. Other Ford advertisements for the Zephyr made it clear that the choice of car was a joint and equal one, and Morris employed a similar theme, albeit with a rather twee catchphrase. But these were beacons of lights in relative darkness.

In the fifties it was no longer necessary to be physically strong to drive a large car safely. With light steering and efficient brakes, even limousines could for the most part be driven by slightly built men and women without exhaustion. But the upmarket and "traditional" makers pandered to contemporary prejudice with abandon. It was to be some time before professional women in large numbers bought their own cars, and, mindful of this, the advertisers frequently limited their involvement to ephemeral matters of fabric choice, colour and gadgets.

Daimler introduced a "Ladies Model" of the One O Four saloon, which came with a telescopic umbrella, power windows, a plated instrument panel and various other fripperies. In many "his and hers" pieces, the man was persuaded with details of performance and mechanical features, while the woman was reassured that the car was "handy" which could mean almost anything. Where women were allowed freer reign, while being no less patronized, was in relation to very small cars (which might be second cars). This particular area is a good example of the car advertisement as indicator of the social mores of the time; motorcars, like other consumer products, are never advertised in a social vacuum, and contemporary advertisements can tell the historian much more than merely the specification of some long forgotten saloon.

While women were enjoined to collude gratefully with the stereotyping, and to accept anything that might be put in front of them, road testers and professional drivers were allowed to be more critical. But even independent tests by the motoring papers could, by modern standards, be surprisingly polite, and, no doubt with advertising revenue firmly in mind, testers were reluctant to be categorically damning of even a questionable product. Frequently, if a car was bad, it was merely stated to have perhaps been designed with priorities other than those of the tester in mind, and the reader was left to work out how many 5′6″ motorists who never drove over forty miles per hour there were for whom the car might be ideally suited!

The result of this gentlemanly restraint was that tests could be quoted in advertisements even for distinctly mediocre cars. The Morris Oxford of the early fifties was painfully slow, and was advertised, quoting a contemporary road test, as having acceleration that was "designed for cruising", and this was implied to be an advantage. Reading between the lines, it was clear that the car took a long time to reach cruising speed, and that it was therefore as well not to have to slow down if that could be avoided.

Ford were luckier, and did not have to scrape the barrel so vigorously. A piece for their large car range of the early fifties consisted almost entirely of quotations from road tests by both of the major motoring weeklies, and the majority of comments were genuinely favourable. Such comprehensive praise was unusual, however, and Ford made the most of it while others dug up ambiguous remarks from a desert of equivocation. Generally, one or two favourable snippets were used, in the hope that their effect would, in the mind of the reader, percolate through to his perception of the rest of the car. "Knocking copy" did not really feature in the fifties, and sideswipes by one maker at another would be subtle, and were usually avoided. The relationship between road tester and advertiser could occasionally be strained, as an unusually unflattering review of the 1957 Vauxhall Victor led Vauxhall to cancel their advertising in a magazine for several months. It was noticeable that an equivalent test in a rival magazine, while not entirely uncritical, was nevertheless more circumspect . . .

Other testimonials could be more subjective. A Hillman Minx advertisement from 1952 cited happy foreign buyers, using proper quoted comments. Austin, with their Hereford, invented a Greek chorus of mythical owners who were unanimous in their delight at the new car. The approach was not confined to that firm. Wolseley inevitably employed the genre, in relation to the 1952 6/80, though they made no pretence that the admirers were real individuals; they were rather implausible stereotypes talking to each other over the roof of the car about the impression it made. Riley employed corny badinage too, although it could be more amusing than most of its kind.

Competition successes were always welcome, and Monte Carlo wins were plugged mercilessly. Ford were able to capitalise on success in 1953, and thus strengthened the enthusiast appeal of their Zephyr, a car which did not appear ideal for rallying until one considered the virtues of its relative power, simplicity and good ground clearance.

Sunbeam-Talbot were similarly able to invite enthusiastic drivers to sample their Alpine and 90 saloon. MG were disingenuous in a 1955 depiction of the MGA sports car, proclaiming it as "1st", and only in the small print explaining that its priority did not rest in any actual success, but in its potential . . .

Austin adopted a novel approach, testing A40s of various kinds, and breaking records with an Atlantic Convertible in the United States. The A40s sold well, though one wonders whether they might have done so anyway, but the Atlantic was a flop, whose engine alone was to rise from the ashes of American disdain in the Austin-Healey 100, a good car which did enjoy considerable competition success and popularity.

An aspect of car advertising during the fifties which cannot go unmentioned is that wonderful and rich reserve of the unimaginative copywriter, the cliché. The cliché can be used to sum up the virtues of the product, as product, but it can also, if carefully selected, be cynically employed to ingratiate the vehicle into the affections of the target market. The approach, examples of which have been seen above, is as old as advertising itself, and most certainly is not confined to motorcars, but the car has such a wide influence on so many aspects of the life of its owner that it has provided an almost unrivalled field for the mangled truism to flourish.

The cliché as motif may be timeless, but individual examples are very much of their period and social context. There is possibly no better example of caricatured use of the cliché than provided by Wolseley, who developed a habit of making unusually explicit what for the most part was decorously hinted at. At the time, such advertisements were overstated, but, decades later, they are hilarious. As in so many things, society moves on, and the advertisers, who highlight and exaggerate transitory social preoccupations, are preserved, petrified in comic pose.

The cliché could be a word, or a phrase, or an attitude. In many cases, all three went together, as in the case of Humber. Fatuous little phrases such as "handsome is as handsome does" were put through the copywriter's mangle, and do not stand up well to the perspective of later years. By the mid-sixties, they had been superseded. Ironically, very early postwar advertisements for Humber are much more appealing, not only for delightful artwork, but for their terse commentary and relatively sober claims.

Many clichés were more subtle – embodying ways of thinking rather than particular phrases – and they were consequently less nauseous than Humber's; while remaining identifiably of their era, they are less immediately risible. Contemporary attitudes in a more general sense are noticeable in relation to advertisers' views both of the family and of contemporary political atmosphere. It was always useful to portray the car as "part of the family", and as a prime contributor to its well-being. In the later part of our period especially, when many families who had not previously owned a car were contemplating one, Standard, Austin, Hillman and Morris filled up their cars with mother, children and dog to convince the potential buyer that a car was worth buying *per se*, and that their products were the most suitable. At the more exalted level of the upper-market car, the point was not so necessary, as car ownership was not a novelty. Ford to some extent eschewed this approach; their advertising for the smaller cars did not rely on too many props at first, though later that would change. When the family started to go abroad for holidays, the car would follow too, and would thus increasingly be portrayed not only as an accessory to the daily grind, but as a means of escaping it.

Contemporary politics and social changes – inevitably enmeshed with general attitudes and standards of living – were reflected in publicity material for cars, as for other consumer goods. During the fifties, colonial references in advertisements petered out. The relative austerity of the early post-war years meant that fun, escapism and abandoning of cares in search of the free, open road were not prominent themes. The country was busy rebuilding itself, exports were a priority, and with food and fuel rationing still in mind it was enough to be given relative peace and security. And while petrol rationing still persisted, few people were likely to be able to escape very far, anyway. Thus portraits of the cars could be earnest, with the driver and passengers soberly dressed, enjoying low-key business or pleasure activities.

Few young people could afford a new car, and so the archetypal driver was a man in his forties. As the fifties drew to a close, and Stafford Cripps' famous slogan, ''Export or die'' was superseded in the public mind by notions of continous expansion and improvement (Macmillan's ''Most of our people have never had it so good'', etc), references to export markets dwindled with the colonial depictions, and suggestions of fun and frivolity, at home and abroad, gained ground.

People were able to enjoy freedom more easily, without being reminded by piles of rubble of how close they had been to losing it, and this relaxation of outlook was apparent in advertising as elsewhere. Moreover, several factors meant that the copywriters had to try harder. The inception of commercial television in 1955 gave the written advertisement a new challenge, and it was vital, in a period when a car had to sell in large numbers to be economic, to gain as large a share of the expanding home market as possible. Once-captive export markets were now looking not only to Britain for new cars, and thus could not be relied upon to take whatever the home market did not want. One of the last instances of the operation of that doctrine was the Vauxhall Victor, for whose export success the company had good reason to be grateful, given the ambivalent reception accorded the car at home. In future, the risk could not be taken. By the end of the fifties, a new régime was beginning to bite.

An interesting development was the advance of the small car which was proud to be small. The idea that someone might actually want a small vehicle, rather than be forced into it by financial exigencies, gradually gained favour, to the extent that the artistic ''elongator'' who, in the early fifties, would add several feet to an economy car in the quest for glamour, was made largely redundant by the end of the decade. Optimistic postwar predictions that small cars would gradually be phased out proved ill-founded. Even in America, imported small cars gained a loyal following. The Suez crisis reminded people that even in peacetime, conflict abroad could endanger fuel supplies, and that the motorist might be held to ransom. That crisis did not last long, and the resultant spate of bubble-cars was shortlived, but small cars continued to sell well.

More persistent factors which contributed to the rise in popularity of the small car were overcrowding in cities which had not been built to cope with the huge rise in car numbers, and the advent of the ''second car'' favoured by suburban commuters. The commuter car did not need to be large, as its duties were largely performed in those areas of confined space – the towns. Small cars were thus increasingly seen either as ancillary transport (by the well-off), or as genuine substitutes for larger vehicles, and were frequently bought by those who could afford something bigger if they chose. This trend belongs more properly to the sixties, but its beginnings, indicated by the emergence of ''deluxe'' editions of utility models, lay in the previous decade.

From the perspective of many decades later, motor-car advertisements from the fifties can seem old-fashioned, funny, or, in some cases, inspired. They are interesting because they reveal what sales figures and technical data alone cannot reveal – how the manufacturers intended their cars to fit into the society and the market of the time. They were aimed at widely differing markets, even within a given price range. There was much rivalry, for instance, between Morris and Austin, and buyers of one would often be quite irrationally reluctant to change to the other.

Old marque loyalties survived well into the sixties, and sometimes beyond. It was not surprising that, in the main, people who would look forward to ''High jinks in a Hillman Minx'' would not be encountered fighting Charles and Giles outside the Wolseley showroom for the latest home market allocation.

An account of British motoring during the early postwar years would be incomplete without the successful, unsuccessful and occasionally bizarre pieces of copy with which manufacturers tried to persuade a fickle public to buy their latest wares.

Double life of a *Sapphire*

FOR HIM

Get behind the wheel of the amazing Sapphire and enjoy yourself. Surging acceleration through the gears to 50 m.p.h. in 8.9 seconds. Up to 75 m.p.h. in third in uncanny silence. Around the 100 mark in top, which means you cruise in the seventies with the 150 b.h.p. twin carburetter engine purring contentedly. Yet, surprisingly, for all this tremendous performance, the Sapphire gives you 22 miles per gallon.

Brakes match the power at your command. Cornering is safe and sweet with special stabilisers preventing all roll. Centrifugal clutch and pre-selectric gears give you a new sense of control and relaxation.

From its unobtrusive good looks to the smallest detail of its appointments, the Sapphire is worthy of its engine, designed and built alongside the famous Sapphire jets, which power the world's finest aircraft. The Gloster Javelin; the Hawker Hunter; the Vulcan; the Victor; and in the U.S.A., the B.57; the F.J.3 Fury and the Republic Thunderstreak.

FOR HER

What a joy it is to go in the Sapphire. So dignified and elegant. Such graceful sweeping lines to excite everyone's admiration. The perfect setting for your entrances and leave-takings.

For luxury travelling the Sapphire stands apart. Quiet as a siesta. Superlatively comfortable, with spacious pile carpeted floors, walnut panelling and every smallest detail carefully considered to add to your well-being.

If you like to drive, the Sapphire will surprise you even more. Front seat adjustable at finger touch. Clear all-round view. And handling with responsiveness and ease that is sheer delight.

Write to Armstrong Siddeley Motors, Ltd., Coventry for fully descriptive catalogue No. S25.

The amazing ARMSTRONG SIDDELEY SAPPHIRE

Single carburetter, synchro gears £1,722 including tax. Twin carburetter and pre-selectric gearbox optional extras.

MEMBER OF THE HAWKER SIDDELEY GROUP

Armstrong Siddeley Sapphire

An attractive advertisement from June 1954 for an elegant luxury car. The advertisement is unusual for the period in its use of colour photographs rather than paintings, but the segregation of male and female priorities is very much the early fifties norm. The copy is relatively modest, with details of features taking priority over the hyperbole favoured by some other makers. It would be a wealthy person indeed who could afford such a car. The styling represents a good compromise between traditional and modern themes.

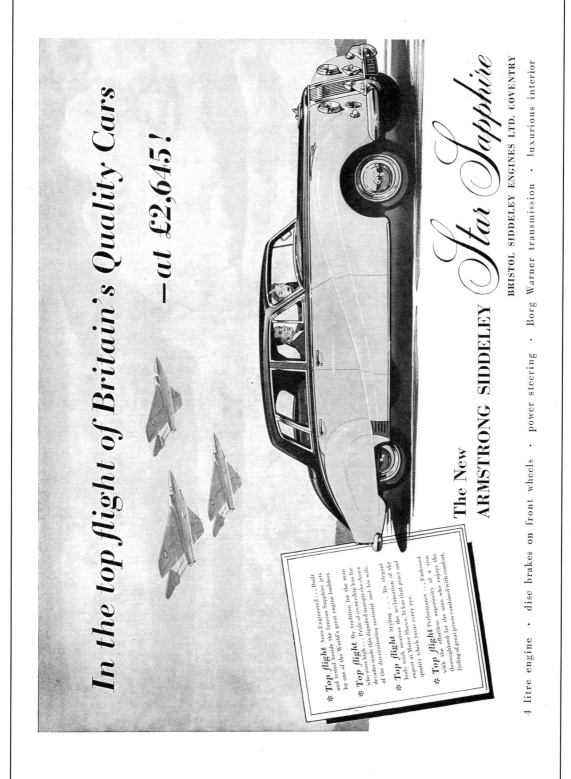

Armstrong Siddeley Star Sapphire

By March 1959, car production by the firm was coming to a close, but the Sapphire had been modernised with cutaway wheel spats, front-hinged doors and other improvements. The aeronautical connections of the maker are used to full affect, with all their connotations of precise engineering and construction, technological prowess and, of course, glamour.

THE AUSTIN *Sheerline*....

A CAR OF DISTINCTION IN ANY SURROUNDINGS

GRACE IN THE COUNTRY. *The silent Sheerline keeps the peace of the country lanes. There is luxurious comfort for passengers and plenty of room for luggage, golf clubs or a picnic hamper for the point-to-point.*

AUTHORITY IN TOWN. *The Sheerline is conservatively distinguished. Its speed and efficiency impress wherever it takes you.*

THE Austin Sheerline is a car which makes an immediate appeal to the man who appreciates a fine piece of precision engineering. Everything about the Sheerline is in the best British tradition of craftsmanship and design. This is a car which quietly and unobtrusively caters in every way for the comfort and convenience of the critical motorist.

Among the many Sheerline luxuries are :— 125 b.h.p. O.H.V. 6-cylinder engine ; hypoid rear axle giving flat floor ; radio ; fresh air heating ; walnut veneer panelling ; generous armchair seating, upholstered in finest leather.

POWER ON TOUR. *The Sheerline is made for the motorist who likes to travel fast and far. It has the power and comfort that make it a pleasure to go on tour.*

AUSTIN —you can depend on it!

THE AUSTIN MOTOR COMPANY LIMITED · LONGBRIDGE · BIRMINGHAM

Austin Sheerline

The potential client is rather baldly flattered here with the description, "critical motorist", which will bolster any sneaking suspicion he may have that lesser mortals might only, if they had the discrimination, forsake less distinguished breeds. The styling did have "authority", but it somehow managed to look rather austere and official, lacking a coachbuilt feel. The other disadvantage was the social ambiguity of the Austin name. Thus it is perhaps not surprising that many were bought as hire cars and for official transportation.

AUSTIN A30 SEVEN
2 or 4 doors. Over 60 m.p.h.,
over 40 m.p.g. Room for four (or
two adults and three children)
plus luggage.

Austin beauty is more than skin deep

THE gleaming beauty of an Austin is more than skin deep. It's *seven* skins deep ! For every Austin gets seven finishes before it leaves the production line (besides the bitumastic applied to some parts for sound insulation).

First, the 'bonderising'—a chemical process that impregnates the steel body surface and protects it against rust from stem to stern, inside and out. Then a dip coat of primer. Then two coats of orange primer. Next a special ' filler ' coat. Finally two coats of glossy enamel, oven-baked for hardness. Result : a lustrous sheen that stays new-looking for years.

What does it cost ? Add to these seven main processes the many intermediate steps: rinsing, 'scuffing', oven-drying, dust-sealing. Then consider the cost. Nearly a million pounds are invested in the huge Roto-dip and paint plants at Longbridge. Machinery moves the car bodies smoothly through these plants. Rinsing, dipping, drying and baking take place automatically.

And the point of it all—Why all this care and trouble ? Why this lavish equipment ? It is done to make sure every Austin is a superb job. To give every Austin owner a car that will go on looking showroom fresh for years.

TO TEST THE SEVEN SKINS

Every batch of paint that forms part of the seven skins of an Austin is put through a merciless investigation. At Longbridge are Humidity Chambers that simulate the worst conditions encountered out of doors — the repeated heavy dews of the tropics — and weatherometers that produce concentrated sunshine. In these ' torture chambers ' the ravages of years are compressed into weeks. Paint that survives is not merely pretty — it's pretty good !

AUSTIN
—you can depend on it !

REMEMBER — *Quality and dependability are guaranteed by the B.M.C. Used-Car Warranty and you are certain of a good deal when you sell.*

THE AUSTIN MOTOR COMPANY LIMITED • LONGBRIDGE • BIRMINGHAM

Austin A30

Solid virtue forms the bedrock of this 1955 piece for the little A30, rival to the Morris Minor, and well liked for its light yet sturdy construction. This example, which is a 1952 model, has been elongated considerably by the artist, in the fashion of the time. These cars lasted well, but had a nasty habit of rolling over if handled clumsily at speed, a trait borne of the required compact dimensions, and inherited from the original Austin Seven.

Everybody's saying it!

THE AUSTIN A70 HEREFORD

is a winner!

"In short, most things that an owner is likely to want have been thought of—and most of them have been thought of in a very sensible way. Coupled with the roadworthiness and comfort mentioned earlier, the sturdy build and attractive price, these things all go to make up a car which must be regarded as a very notable model indeed in its class."

—from an independent road test by the 'Motor'.

Passengers say . . .

'. . . for such a high performance car the A70 has lots of room inside. It's quite comfortable with three in the back and there's plenty of leg room. You get a wonderfully smooth ride over any road.'

'. . . those deep seats—upholstered in real leather—are a joy; the big windows are also a very good feature.'

Drivers say . . .

'. . . it has a splendid performance. The 68 b.h.p. overhead valve engine really pushes out the power and the car corners at speed as if it were on rails.'

'The independent front suspension, steering-column gear change and four-wheel hydraulic braking help to make driving the Hereford a wonderful experience.'

Passers-by say . . .

'. . . isn't that Austin a beauty? Those wide rear-opening doors are very convenient . . . and the luggage compartment looks very spacious.'

'. . . easy to handle and park, by the look of it. Nice solidly built jobs . . . they say Austins last for years. And they're very economical too.'

Austin say . . .

Austins are Britain's best-selling cars. They're reliable, economical and have an excellent performance. There are Austin Dealers in practically every town throughout the country. They will be happy to tell you all about the Austin A70 Hereford. NOW is the time to ask.

AUSTIN

—you can
depend on it!

THE AUSTIN MOTOR COMPANY LIMITED • LONGBRIDGE • BIRMINGHAM

Austin A70 Hereford

"In short, most things have been thought of", in a "notable" model. The praise is somewhat lukewarm from "The Motor", especially for 1952, when road tests of the most appalling heaps tended to be polite about questionable habits. Even Austin say that the car is "quite" comfortable, though that "quite" is most likely a mannerism, rather than a qualification. Passers-by talk in a very stilted way, and the drivers, apart from all saying the same thing, sound almost as if they are reading a script. Never . . . !

EQUATOR TO ARCTIC CIRCLE

★

8,000 gruelling miles in 11½ days

Austin A40 makes epic day-and-night dash

ON SATURDAY, MARCH 28th, after 11 days 10 hours, an Austin A40 completed the most arduous journey in motoring history. From the heat of the Equator to the cold of the Arctic, it had covered 8,000 miles across some of the worst country in the world — through torrid jungles, across pitiless deserts, over frozen wastes.

A sensational drive. And a sensational car!

THIS WAS THE ROUTE

Why was the journey made?
The purpose of this journey was to find the answers to a number of scientific problems connected with developments in the suspension and cooling systems on future Austins.

No laboratory experiment could provide a test like this—only an actual high-speed run from intense heat to intense cold. The A40 carried special instruments so that the car's performance could be watched and logged under the most punishing motoring conditions ever experienced.

Austin leads the way.
It was an Austin that went round the world in 21 days. It was an Austin that covered 10,000 miles in 10,000 minutes. Austins are constantly being put to the most gruelling tests—and coming through with flying colours.

The aim? To give Austins still finer performance; still greater stamina. To give motorists still better Austins.

The drivers were :

ALAN HESS · KEN WHARTON · RON JEAVONS

ANOTHER GREAT **AUSTIN** ACHIEVEMENT!

Austin A40 Somerset

If you happen to be planning an 8000 mile round trip, choose an Austin. The company organised a number of these exploits, particularly with the A90 coupe, in America. These exercises did not help the A90 Atlantic, and may or may not have helped the Somerset. The car was very rugged, and a separate chassis made body corrosion less critical. The "epic journey" theme was unusual in post-war advertising, though it complemented Austin's already established reputation for reliability.

> TO PLEASE *today's motorist, stylist and designer get down to the subtle blending of the car's colours inside and out.*

Woman consultant chooses materials and colours for new Austin Cambridge

WHEN you buy an Austin you buy more than fine engineering and design; more than the most dependable car in its price range. For Austin employ experts to finish the job supremely well; right down to the subtle blending of the car's colours, inside and out.

Take the new Austin Cambridge. You have many attractive colour schemes to choose from. And a woman devised them — Mrs. Kay Petre, colour adviser to the Austin Motor Company and famous racing driver.

She advises on the materials and colours to be used. Each material is carefully chosen to do its job best : for the seats, material with years of wear in it; for the floor, thick strong carpeting; for doors, pockets, shelves, special long-lasting coverings.

And the colour of each is chosen to create harmony, to tone with the rest, to match up with the outside of the car. Always she works in close consultation with the stylists and designers.

Harmony inside and out

Kay Petre has decided on the materials, and on the colours. Now she and the designer see how the scheme looks in the car, whether it goes well with the outside finish. For every exterior colour needs a matching interior combination.

Cambridge Prices from £458 plus £191.19.2d. p.t. Austin Dealers have full details.

AUSTIN
— you can depend on it!

REMEMBER—
Quality and dependability are guaranteed by the B.M.C. Used-Car Warranty and you are certain of a good deal when you sell.

THE AUSTIN MOTOR COMPANY LIMITED · LONGBRIDGE · BIRMINGHAM

Austin Cambridge

An unusual angle on the new-look Cambridge. Kay Petre makes the choice of colour explicitly human, rather than an accident of industrial fate. No doubt it pleased those who wished to feel that someone had troubled over their tastes. The theme foreshadows the "designer" fetish of later years. The elaborately painted hubcaps were not standard equipment, but the car was nevertheless elegant and modern for its time.

The car so many people are so very proud to own!

THE AUSTIN A90 SIX WESTMINSTER. Big. Fast. Stylish. With a near-silent 2.6 litre six-cylinder O.H.V. engine that will give a true 90 m.p.h. OVERDRIVE is available as an optional extra to give refined performance and more m.p.g.

Fittings, lines and comfort are in the luxury class. A huge boot takes the family luggage and more.

Here is a car that makes travel both enjoyable and exciting. A car to be proud of. Like the A30 Seven and A40-A50 Cambridge, it's a true-blooded Austin.

REMEMBER—Quality and dependability are guaranteed by the B.M.C. Used-Car Warranty and you are certain of a good deal when you sell.

Appointment to Her Majesty
Queen Elizabeth II
Motor Car Manufacturers,
The Austin Motor Company Limited

AUSTIN

— you can depend on it!

THE AUSTIN MOTOR COMPANY LIMITED · LONGBRIDGE · BIRMINGHAM

Austin A90 Westminster

Prestige overtly enters the equation with the larger, six-cylinder model in the Austin range. In spite of appearances, it is substantially larger than the Cambridge, and is obviously wider. The chrome sideflash is a distinguishing touch. The setting is deliberately upmarket, although those midgets inside the car might have some difficulty in mounting the fullsize horses . . .

YOU
AND YOUR OTHER SELF
AGREE
on the
AUSTIN A40

Half of you wants a sleek-lined temptress of a car. A car that exultantly matches you mood for mood on the open road, a car that still looks adventurous in the most adventurous holiday spots. **In fact — the Austin A40.** Half of you wants a car that's formal and perfect (not too formal but very perfect) in any setting. A car so sleek and exciting in design and conception it makes others look pompous. **In fact — the Austin A40.** All of you wants a car that will on any occasion take you clean out of the rut of run-of-the-mill motoring ; a car as personal as the clothes you wear. **In fact — the Austin A40.**

HOW COME ?

The secret of the A40's dual-personality lies in its superb engineering and design. It's got shapely stunning good looks. It's got space for four real life-size adults inside — and above all room in the boot (simply by laying the rear seat flat you double the boot-space). And it gives you real surging power on a shoestring. Take a trip to your local Austin dealer and inspect the A40's specification. Price £638.12.6 (£450 plus £183.12.6 P.T.)

GET INTO AN AUSTIN AND OUT OF THE ORDINARY !

By Appointment to
Her Majesty The Queen
Motor Car Manufacturers
The Austin Motor
Company Limited

Backed by
BMC 12-month
warranty
and BMC
service

THE AUSTIN MOTOR COMPANY LIMITED
LONGBRIDGE · BIRMINGHAM

Austin A40 Mk 1

A radical change of image follows a change of designer; in this case, Pininfarina of Italy was consulted in the styling of the 1958 A40, which looked not at all like previous small Austins. No doubt £638 12s 6d was a worthwhile price to pay to avoid terminal schizophrenia. BMC are visibly trying to rid Austin of an earlier, stolid pipe-and-slippers image; to some extent the attempt was successful.

GET INTO AN AUSTIN AND OUT OF THE ORDINARY !

You hear the quick, distant beat of hooves on the ground. The still air trembles. You stop the car. And away in the distance you see the first sharp outline of racehorses cantering by.

A pleasant surprise? Certainly. But then life with the Austin A99 is always pleasant. For here is a car that is everything you want a car to be. It spirits you away at 100 mph and more: responds to your wishes with effortless ease. It is powerful: it is obedient: it has the quiet assurance of a true-born thoroughbred. The simple restraint of the styling is a constant delight to the eye. The comfort inside, a clear invitation to a life of luxury. This is the Austin A99. A car that makes life very sweet and motoring happy and carefree again.

Austin A99: 2.9 litres, 2912 ccs, overdrive, Disc brakes

THE AUSTIN MOTOR COMPANY LIMITED · LONGBRIDGE · BIRMINGHAM

Austin A99 Westminster

A fresh outlook for the prestige model of the range, too. Pininfarina has been at work again, but the styling, with prominent fins, is arguably more cumbersome than that of rival offerings from Ford and Vauxhall. Dependability is here unmentioned; racier virtues have come to the fore. But racy handling was denied the car, though in this class that hardly mattered.

JUST TRY TO FIND THE 'ORDINARY' IN AN AUSTIN SEVEN

The Austin Seven has four wheels (five, if you count the spare). But there the resemblance to an ordinary car stops. ■ Ordinary cars don't double their size the moment you get inside—the Austin Seven does (it's the largest, roomiest car ever packed into ten tiny feet). ■ Ordinary cars don't have the engine mounted sideways —the Austin Seven does. ■ Ordinary cars don't have front-wheel drive—the Austin Seven does. ■ Ordinary cars don't have all-round independent suspension—the Austin Seven does. ■ Ordinary cars do have a transmission shaft—the Austin Seven doesn't. ■ Ordinary cars do have a rear axle—the Austin Seven doesn't.■Ordinary cars . . . but why go on? From bumper to bumper this car is pure revolution.

GET INTO AN AUSTIN AND OUT OF THE ORDINARY !

BUT BE WARNED!
The Austin Seven isn't everyone's car. It's for those who don't mind being in the centre of things the focus of interest for the car-curious of all ages. It's for people who enjoy showing other people under the bonnet, and under the back seat. Where the luggage goes. And how the miles go! It's for people who never get bored with the endless questions about (a) how fast it will go, (b) how many miles it will do to a gallon, and (c) how much it costs. (Your Austin dealer will tell you that the answers are (a) over 70 mph, (b) up to 50 mpg, and (c) under £500.*)

*£350, plus £146.19.2 P.T.

By Appointment to
Her Majesty The Queen
Motor Car Manufacturers
The Austin Motor
Company Limited

Backed by
BMC 12-month
warranty
and BMC
service

BUY BRITISH—BY BMC
THE AUSTIN MOTOR COMPANY LIMITED
LONGBRIDGE · BIRMINGHAM

Austin Seven Mini

Unashamedly extrovert advertising for the Mini, bringing Austin into a market which would not give houseroom to a Hereford. It was pure revolution, too, as a look at the technical features reveals. The girl in the spotty jumper is perhaps brushing water off her boot from the boot of the car; early Minis were plagued by leaks, which an embarrassed BMC eventually traced to incorrect panel welding. This 1959 debutante marked a turning point in small car design.

BEAUTIFULLY FAST,
THE AUSTIN HEALEY

Shirt and Accessories by Woollands of Knightsbridge

This is an unusual picture. It shows an Austin Healey at rest; and that is one thing this magnificent sports car rarely is. For when you think of an Austin Healey, you think of beauty in action. You think of an immensely powerful sports car going ahead like streak lightning. You think of a speedometer that goes 70 . . . 80 . . . 90 . . . 100 — and more. You think of the sheer excitement and exhilaration of being at the wheel of a record-breaker.

But the Austin Healey is not only beautiful to watch and beautiful to drive. The car itself is a beautiful engineering and design job. Its surging power comes from a superb 2.6 litre O.H.V. engine. Its wonderfully finished body is built on aerodynamic lines for speed. Its controls (one of the results of racing experience) are handily placed for sports driving. Its boot is particularly large for this kind of car. One final word. The upholstery is real leather, the carpeting is luxurious, the accessories are part and parcel of the standard equipment. Considering all this and the class of the car, the price of the Austin Healey is remarkably reasonable : £806 plus £404 7s. P.T.

AUSTIN HEALEY

The Austin Motor Company Limited, Longbridge, Birmingham

Austin-Healey 100

An evocative presentation of the Austin-Healey 100 from 1956. Racing experience is always worth plugging, and a low-slung exhaust which always grounded on bumps did not put off the buyers. The 2.6-litre engine originally came from the Austin Atlantic, a neo-Buick that the British thought big and vulgar, and which the Americans thought small and silly. The Americans loved this one, though, and it brought in a good share of much-needed foreign currency.

Take a

BENTLEY

into partnership

Bentley R-type Standard Steel Saloon

The pursuit of excellence possessed a quasi-moral character, and so the Bentley, as an excellent car, was also supposed to serve as a symbol of British pre-eminence. In spite of this possible interpretation of the car, many who were in a position to buy such vehicles eschewed them in favour of more discreet transport.

BENTLEY
'S' SERIES

*A new motor car representing a logical advance
in the design of chassis and coachwork.*

Bentley S Series Saloon

*The date is 1956, and the styling of the Standard Steel Bentley progresses from 1941 to 1947. The
background is again industrial. Bentley were one of the few makers who did not require their copywriters to
wax lyrical about their products – the reputation went ahead. This S1 has "factory" bodywork; a minority of
cars were still fitted with bespoke coachwork from various sources. The styling of this body took some
beating. Alas, so did the rust on neglected, high mileage examples.*

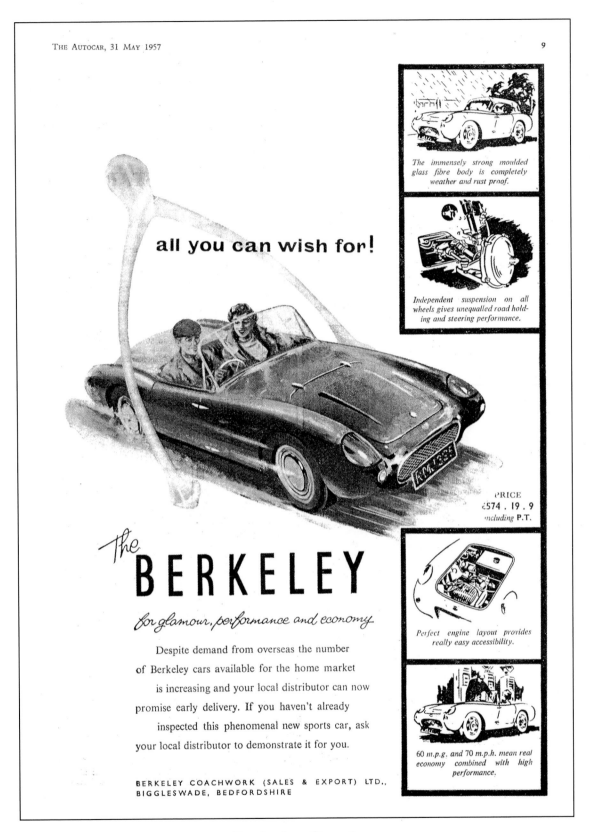

all you can wish for!

The immensely strong moulded glass fibre body is completely weather and rust proof.

Independent suspension on all wheels gives unequalled road holding and steering performance.

PRICE
£574 . 19 . 9
including P.T.

The **BERKELEY**

for glamour, performance and economy

Despite demand from overseas the number of Berkeley cars available for the home market is increasing and your local distributor can now promise early delivery. If you haven't already inspected this phenomenal new sports car, ask your local distributor to demonstrate it for you.

BERKELEY COACHWORK (SALES & EXPORT) LTD., BIGGLESWADE, BEDFORDSHIRE

Perfect engine layout provides really easy accessibility.

60 m.p.g. and 70 m.p.h. mean real economy combined with high performance.

Berkeley Sports

Cleverly advertised in the manner of a conventional sports car, the Berkeley owed much to motorcycle technology with its 328cc engine, and straight-gate gearchange. The glassfibre body, an avant-garde feature for 1957, combined strength with the lightness necessary with such a small engine. For a few years during the middle and late fifties, a huge variety of very small cars was available to British buyers, though increasing affluence and the stabilisation of fuel availability and prices mitigated against many of them in the long term.

Bond Minicar Mk C

Although the best-known micro-cars originated abroad, several British manufacturers offered minimal motoring with varying degrees of success. The original Bond Minicar was made for many years before the Suez crisis gave such devices a sales boost, and the Bond was among the most successful. This Mk C with separate front wings looked more like a "real" car than the original, and the advertisement concentrates on persuading the sceptic that the Bond really does do the work of a conventional car at minimum cost.

Painted by THEYRE LEE-ELLIOTT for The Daimler Company

Grace of movement, masterly technique that captures the very spirit of the dance . . . such qualities we admire in the ballerina's art. The 'Consort', too, we praise for its mastery of motion. Built to the exacting Daimler standards of luxury and elegance, it is the most pleasant and restful of cars to drive at speed, yet at the same time surprisingly agile in traffic. For the man with a position to keep up, for the firm with its prestige to consider, the Daimler 'Consort' is the perfect choice . . . . a car to be proud of for years to come.

THE DAIMLER 'CONSORT'

BY APPOINTMENT
The Daimler Co. Limited
Motor Car Manufacturers
To the late King George VI

Daimler Consort

Not for Daimler the precise statistic. A Daimler carried with it an aura of grace and refinement, an impression enhanced by Royal favour over the years. This advertisement from 1952 attempts to install the Consort into the annals of British Tradition, but the attempt is embarrassingly contrived. The "we" could either refer to the Daimler Company, which would be subjective praise even by the standards of 1952, or to the public, which would be impossibly patronizing! The car itself, however, was well-made, if conservative in appearance, and in a few years the Dowager presence would make way for something more forward-looking.

"Chelsea Flower Show" painted by VICTOR GALLIANO

Tall lupins, proud lilies, aristocrats of the rose garden . . . every flower under these broad awnings

is the crowning achievement of the gardener's patient devotion and skill. In the same way, one car epitomises

the finest traditions of British craftsmanship. As English as the rose . . . designed with the

thoroughness that is satisfied with nothing short of perfection . . .

it's undoubtedly a Daimler

BY APPOINTMENT
The Daimler Co. Limited
Motor Car Manufacturers
To the late King George VI

The Daimler 'Regency'

the 3 litre, 90 b.h.p. Daimler, new in chassis,
engine and body design; with spacious comfort
for six—a car of outstanding character.

Daimler Regency

With painful reluctance, Daimler allows the front wings to blend into the doors of the new style, and 1942 Oldsmobile takes over from English Perpendicular. Though forced onto an essentially alien background, the traditional grille does not look out of place, owing to clever curvature of the shell in sympathy with the front wings. The copy is no longer gauche, but the advertisement as a whole has a naïveté which could not survive long in the marketing climate of a postwar world.

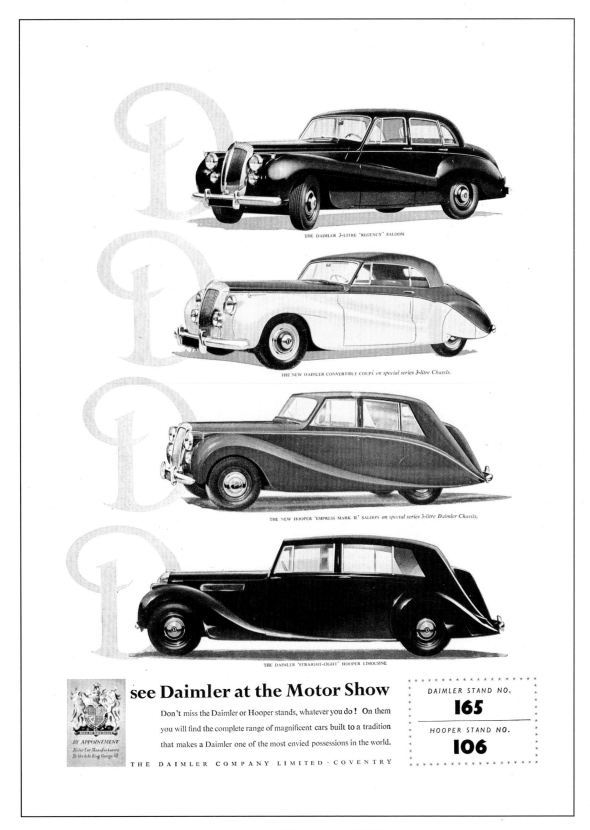

THE DAIMLER 3-LITRE 'REGENCY' SALOON

THE NEW DAIMLER CONVERTIBLE COUPÉ *on special series 3-litre Chassis.*

THE NEW HOOPER 'EMPRESS MARK II' SALOON *on special series 3-litre Daimler Chassis.*

THE DAIMLER 'STRAIGHT-EIGHT' HOOPER LIMOUSINE

BY APPOINTMENT
Motor Car Manufacturers
To the late King George VI

see Daimler at the Motor Show

Don't miss the Daimler or Hooper stands, whatever you do ! On them
you will find the complete range of magnificent cars built to a tradition
that makes a Daimler one of the most envied possessions in the world.

THE DAIMLER COMPANY LIMITED · COVENTRY

DAIMLER STAND NO.
165

HOOPER STAND NO.
106

Daimler Range, 1952

A modest offering, leading one up the social scale. The poor Regency looks humbled in this company, and is dwarfed by the huge Straight Eight. The Convertible Coupe, with its two-tone paint, borders on the flashy, and is a taste of things to come. It was crammed with luxury and gadgets, and was more exciting than the Special Sports that it replaced, though arguably less elegant. The annual Motor Show was often used by manufacturers as an opportunity to promote the whole product range in the press.

Great enthusiasm for the new
DAIMLER REGENCY Mk II

THE SWIFT, IMMACULATE CAR FOR MEN OF AFFAIRS

THE RECENT introduction at the Motor Show of the magnificent new Daimler Regency Mk.II has given immense satisfaction to all motorists who have been awaiting a new *big* Daimler. The Regency is undoubtedly a big car—spacious, luxurious and dignified —and of infinite value to the busy man of affairs.

But the Regency's capacity for providing an extremely high degree of comfort for five adults in no way detracts from a remarkable performance, for this aristocrat of a car is also fast and most enjoyably manœuvrable.

Like every Daimler it handles like silk . . . thanks to fluid transmission. The Regency is available with $3\frac{1}{2}$ or $4\frac{1}{2}$ litre engine. The $3\frac{1}{2}$ litre gives a cruising speed of over 70 with a top speed of over 80 mph. The corresponding figures for the $4\frac{1}{2}$ litre are 80 and 90 mph.

The price, too, has met with approval—the inclusive figure of £2324. 9. 2 (for the $3\frac{1}{2}$ litre) being generally considered extremely reasonable for such a car. Also causing great interest are the new *specialist's* $4\frac{1}{2}$ litre Sportsman saloon and the new Daimler 'Regina' 7-seater limousine. **The Regency Mk.II has the new Dunlop Tubeless Tyres fitted as standard equipment.**

'POWER WITH PRESTIGE'

BY APPOINTMENT
The Daimler Co. Limited,
Motor Car Manufacturers
to the late King George VI

THE DAIMLER COMPANY LIMITED · RADFORD WORKS · COVENTRY

Daimler Regency Mk II

An immensely solid car, the new Regency looked very American in shape if one disregarded the grille. The car is portrayed as an asset to the VIP who has regard for his image. The market for such cars was very small, but well-defined. The text, like the car, is restrained and elegant, in marked contrast to the uncouth and turgid prose that was from time to time inflicted on certain other, less distinguished marques.

The universal appeal of the Daimler CONQUEST range

BY APPOINTMENT
The Daimler Co. Limited
Motor Car Manufacturers
to the late King George VI

WHAT an exceptional quartet of cars is the Daimler Conquest range. Look at them individually—there is Daimler dignity, brilliant performance, fluid flywheel transmission, automatic chassis lubrication, a superb standard of craftsmanship in finish. Consider them collectively—where else would you find a range of cars offering such a rare combination of qualities to such widely differing tastes?

The Conquest Saloon. 75 bhp, 80 mph. Acceleration 0-60 in 20.4 secs. Petrol consumption from 26.5 mpg. at 30 to 21 mpg. at 60. £1066 plus £445.5.10 p/t.

The 'Conquest Century'. 100 bhp. Twin carburetters, 0-60 in 16.3 seconds! Bigger brakes, more leg room in rear, telescopic steering, etc. £1172 plus £489.9.2 p/t.

The Conquest Roadster. Over 100 miles an hour! £1180 plus £492.15.10 p/t. Also available in a very attractive alternative body style with a fixed head.

The Conquest Coupé 100 bhp. The folding head is power operated to raise or lower at the touch of a button. £1225 plus £511.10.10 p/t.

THE DAIMLER COMPANY LIMITED · RADFORD WORKS · COVENTRY

Daimler Conquest convertible

By the mid-fifties, Daimler's range was extensive; this version of the "small" Daimler was well regarded, and sold in reasonable numbers for the period. The design of the door locks, folding head and side windows resembled those of the contemporary Ford and Austin convertibles. This was no accident, as Carbodies made them all. It is typical of the period that a woman is allowed to press the switch, while men actually drive the other cars.

'Five-Star' cars are

Exciting *

CONSUL

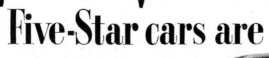

The **Motor** *says...*

PERFORMANCE

ZEPHYR-SIX—
"Outstanding performance . . . the engine turns with really electric motor smoothness . . . will out-accelerate any car in its class."

CONSUL—
"Good all round acceleration . . . very smooth . . . conforms to an acceptable standard of silence."

COMFORT

ZEPHYR-SIX—
"Will carry six people in comfort — with room to spare."

CONSUL—
"The Front suspension is unique . . . an extremely comfortable ride . . . good bump absorption . . . an entire absence of pitch or float."

SAFETY

ZEPHYR-SIX—
"Accurate and sensitive steering . . . potent braking system . . . very safe."

CONSUL—
"Tenacious road holding . . . on corners . . . ease of control . . . the steering is notable for lightness."

STYLE

ZEPHYR-SIX—
"Clean attractive lines . . . fine styling . . . sensible lack of ostentatious decoration."

CONSUL—
"That rare vehicle — an everyman's car that is basically good by any standard."

CONSUL: £470 plus P.T. **£262. 12. 3**

The **Autocar** *says...*

PERFORMANCE

ZEPHYR-SIX—
"A genuine speed of over 80 m.p.h. — will cruise all day between 60 and 70 m.p.h."

CONSUL—
"Full advantage has been taken of modern ideas in design. A quick no-fuss getaway from cold."

COMFORT

ZEPHYR-SIX—
"Roomy without being cumbersome . . . the interior — neat yet business like."

CONSUL—
"The suspension permits very little roll . . . riding is level on average surfaces — severe shock is absorbed."

SAFETY

ZEPHYR-SIX—
"The steering — light and very positive . . . the brakes — powerful yet progressive . . . visibility is extremely good."

CONSUL—
"The car rides extremely well and has powerful brakes . . . steering is fingerlight yet definite."

STYLE

ZEPHYR-SIX—
"A very satisfactory car . . . has a clean external appearance with balance of line."

CONSUL—
"A smart car entirely in the modern style . . . clean lines and a smooth appearance . . . one of the outstanding cars produced since the war in the popular class — has handling qualities that would be acceptable on a car of any price."

ZEPHYR-SIX: £532 plus P.T. **£297. 1. 1**

Greater Value than ever since price reductions

ZEPHYR-SIX

Ford

★ ★ ★ ★ ★

MOTORING

THE BEST AT LOWEST COST

BY APPOINTMENT MOTOR VEHICLE MANUFACTURERS TO THE LATE KING GEORGE VI FORD MOTOR COMPANY LTD.

EARLS COURT · Oct 22nd—Nov 1st · Stand No 137

Ford Consul & Zephyr Mk 1

An interesting example of the "testimonial" approach. This advertisement uses an unusually large number of extracts from the motoring weeklies. Reviews of the large Fords were generally favourable. Although the word "exciting" is used, it is more concerned with excitement through competence than with notions of escape or glamour. The date is October, 1952.

Three cars in one! Two Models!

Three 'Five-Star' Cars in one

The Convertible—the smartest, most useful car so far evolved—is creating new demands for Consul and Zephyr. As convertibles their appearance is dashing —an elegant saloon, a continental coupé de ville or a clean-lined open tourer.

Famous Engines

The Monte-Carlo-Rally-winning six-cylinder unit powers the Zephyr Convertible. The Consul Convertible's four-cylinder engine also runs to a world-wide success.

Power-operated top

The Zephyr's top is power-operated at the touch of a button. The Consul's is hand-controlled but power operation is available as an extra. Both give you open tourer freedom plus protection the moment it rains. And in both the top, when down, disappears completely into the body.

A Delight to Drive

Ford 'GLIDE-RIDE' suspension — space — comfort, control, visibility, Ford-Famous and all here together. And Ford Service, too!

CONSUL CONVERTIBLE: £570 *Plus P.T. £238 . 12 . 6*
ZEPHYR CONVERTIBLE: £677 *Plus P.T. £283 . 4 . 2*

Ford ★ '5-STAR' MOTORING

the best at lowest cost

Ford Zephyr convertible Mk 1

Late 1953 saw the advent of the Consul and Zephyr convertibles, with a power hood on the Zephyr and occasionally on the Consul, too. Competition successes and good service facilities are here given a mention, and it is interesting that Ford does not go into rhapsodies about the joys of the open road in summertime. The power hood operated in a similar manner to that of the Daimler Conquest convertible.

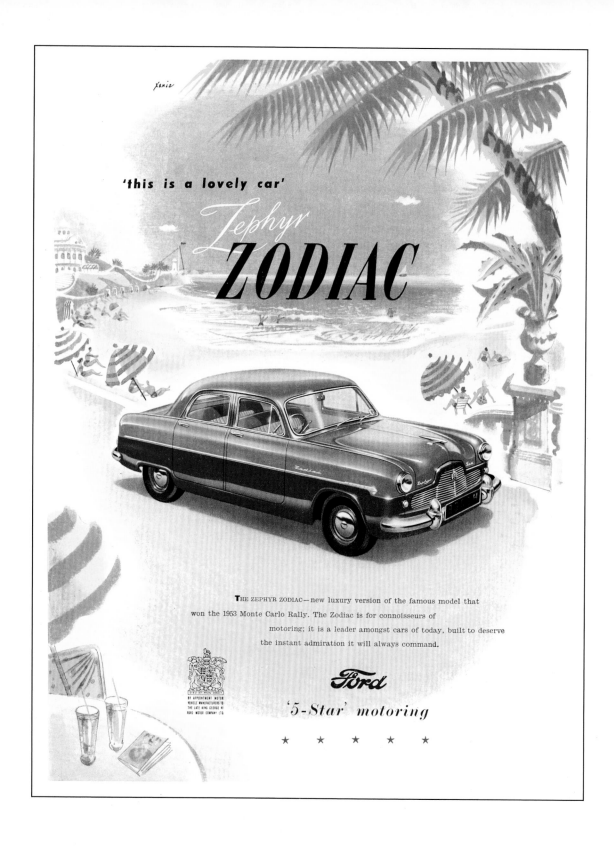

'this is a lovely car'

Zephyr

ZODIAC

THE ZEPHYR ZODIAC—new luxury version of the famous model that won the 1953 Monte Carlo Rally. The Zodiac is for connoisseurs of motoring; it is a leader amongst cars of today, built to deserve the instant admiration it will always command.

Ford

'5-Star' motoring

★ ★ ★ ★ ★

Ford Zephyr Zodiac

A pleasant depiction of a Zodiac in Dorchester Grey and Westminster Blue. This is an upmarket and semi-exotic advertisement, which is some way removed from earlier pieces emphasising the Ford's utility. The Zodiac would increasingly acquire its own identity, and though referred to in Mk 1 form as the "Zephyr Zodiac", the "Zephyr" prefix would later be dropped. The car is interesting as an early example of an emergent marketing theme – the promotion of a deluxe edition of the mainstream saloon as a car with its own distinct image and persona.

The first light cars in the '5-Star' class

new **Prefect**

★ ★ ★ ★ ★

new **Anglia**

★ ★ ★ ★ ★

The new Anglia and new Prefect are beautiful in appearance and seat four big people in comfort. There is unusually large luggage space. These two new cars give really 'big-car' performance, yet ideally balanced power-to-weight ratio ensures low petrol consumption, reduced engine wear and remarkably low running costs. Independent front suspension, as on the famous Zephyr 6 and Consul, provides easiest riding and safest cornering. All-round visibility, hydraulically operated clutch and brakes and all-steel welded integral body make these cars superbly safe. See them at the Motor Show. There is a Ford Dealer at your service in your Town.

**More room
and style
at less
per mile**

Ford **'5-Star' motoring the best at lowest cost**

STAND No. 137 · EARLS COURT

Ford Anglia & Prefect 100E

Modest paintings of up to the minute cars. The new light Fords were a great advance over the old "uprights", and were designed along the lines of the larger Consul/Zephyr range. Three speed gearboxes and vacuum wipers (which stopped when going uphill and sounded like a manic grandfather clock coming down) remained, but flashing turn signals and more direct, high-geared steering were welcome improvements. Ford advertisements were among the most unaffected of the time, but the cars sold well on value and competence alone.

Ford Escort & Squire 100E

New for 1956 were the small estate cars. The Squire, which initially came with wooden strips down the sides, was the better equipped, being roughly equivalent to the Prefect saloon. Neither vehicle was elegant, and this advertisement sensibly does not try to impart streamlining to cars that inevitably look like vans with windows. Wooden decoration on obviously steel station wagons was popular for top of the range Ford and Mercury wagons in the United States, but even mild manifestations of this fad were often derided in Britain.

The New Zodiac

FORD AGAIN SETS THE FASHION
—WITH "THE THREE GRACES"

THE NEW ZODIAC
(6 cylinder) £645 . 0 . 0 PLUS P.T. £323 . 17 . 0

THE NEW ZEPHYR
(6 cylinder) £580 . 0 . 0 PLUS P.T. £291 . 7 . 0

THE NEW CONSUL
(4 cylinder) £520 . 0 . 0 PLUS P.T. £261 . 7 . 0

THE NEW FORD LINE — Breathtakingly beautiful. Each of these three new cars —"The Three Graces"— is distinctively styled. All three set the fashion with the new Ford line, shown here by the new Zodiac. Each is beautifully proportioned to look longer, lower and wider, with a balanced silhouette.

DRIVING IS EASY AND SAFE. Safety is dominant in the design. Wide-vision windscreens and wrap-around rear windows provide clear views of all four corners of the cars. Powerful brakes, strong construction, a small turning circle and balanced weight distribution aid your contribution to road safety.

NEW COMFORT. There's room for 6 in the soft, wide seats. New appointments and beautiful new instrument panels with regrouped controls add to complete relaxation. Ford 'Glide-ride' front suspension and new rear springing cushion passengers and cars. New body colours and upholstery patterns perfect the picture.

SUPERB PERFORMANCE. New, *over-square*, larger capacity engines run sweetly and more economically at lower revolutions. Superb design results in savings in fuel and engine wear with increased 'all-speed' efficiency. Automatic overdrive is also available. **These new cars offer the motoring you dream about at realistic costs.**

See them at your Dealer's

 'FIVE-STAR' MOTORING AND FORD SERVICE TOO

The best at lowest cost

Ford Zodiac Mk 2

A new approach to copy complements a new range of cars, and the cultural reference indicates consolidation of an upmarket position. MacPherson struts, still unique to Ford, provided the "Glide-ride" suspension. These had first been seen on the MacPherson-designed Chevrolet Cadet, a stillborn postwar compact whose narrow potential profit margins did not make it viable. But it is ironic that the "Glide-ride" name had also been used in 1955 Chevrolet publicity for their conventionally suspended Two-Ten Handyman wagon. As a rule, it was the Americans who favoured spurious names for mundane features. Another was Buick's Variable Pitch Dynaflow (transmission) which conjured up all kinds of uncomfortable images.

voyage
of
discovery

Wind favourable...position plotted...everything set very fair. Now all she has to do is take the wheel and they're off—on a voyage of discovery, an earthbound journey into spaciousness! Their means of transport? Consul of course. A six-seating revelation of good looks, luxury and splendour. A car that gives more room to breathe; more comforting thoughts for their comfort; more big-car details than they (or you) would ever have dreamed possible—all for a more-than-modest fare! So: if you think that running a six-seater is an expensive proposition, start your own voyage of discovery. See your nearest Ford Dealer and find out for yourself what a truly remarkable buy the Consul really is—out-of-this-world!

CONSUL DE LUXE

CONSUL from £545 plus £228.4.2 p.t.= £773.4.2 AND UNIQUE WORLD-WIDE  SERVICE TOO!

Ford Consul Mk 2

The new Consul was larger than its predecessor, and sold equally as well. The styling was clearly American inspired, but was spared most of the parent idiom's excesses. This is a "lowline" version, which featured a revised interior, flatter roofline and other small improvements over the 1956 original. The nautical flavour of this advertisement was permissible, as these cars, unlike some others, were not noted for boat-like handling!

HAVE FUN IN THE SUN WITH FORD!

Now's the time to plan your Ford-powered holiday! A motorised caravan perhaps (there are several different types to choose from), or a Dowty Turbocraft — they'll give you your full share of fun in the sun. A Zephyr Convertible (seats five comfortably) or any one of Ford's fine range of 16 models will make your holiday journey a thrill and a delight. Either way, see your Ford Main Dealer now — he'll be happy to help you with all your holiday problems. Whether your choice is a caravan, craft or car, he'll help you plan to get the most out of your annual vacation.

MAKE IT A ⬡F⬡O⬡R⬡D⬡ POWERED HOLIDAY!

266 SPB

Ford Zephyr Mk 2 Convertible

Boats feature again, in a different context. The glamorous convertible was never intended to sell in large numbers, but it was popular among those who wanted a large touring car that could be opened up in the summer, but who did not need or want an upmarket luxury model. It had no direct rival, and was designed along similar lines to the Mk 1. In the background is a Ford Thames.

EXCITING
IN
EXCITING
OUT

The Anglia makes adventurers of us all. Light and lively, swift and sturdy, it urges you to point its nose towards faraway places with exciting possibilities. Fast (up to 75 mph) and frugal (up to 50 mpg), the dashing Anglia's the sportiest of saloons (1-2-3 in its class, African Safari Rally), the roomiest of light cars. There's no car in its class to touch the Anglia for motoring magic—easy hp terms, low insurance rates, fixed-cost service and high re-sale value make it an outstandingly economical investment—and of course it's soundly backed everywhere you go by quality Ford Service, ready to give your Anglia all the care it will ever need.

STANDARD **£589**.0.10 (£415 + £174.0.10 p.t.)	or from £117.16.2 deposit and 36 instalments of £16.0.8 or £250 deposit and 36 instalments of £11.10.9.	DE-LUXE **£610**.5.10 (£430 + £180.5.10 p.t.)

ANGLIA

THE WORLD'S MOST EXCITING LIGHT CAR FROM **F☉RD**

Ford Motor Company Limited, Car & Truck Domestic Division, Cheapside House, 135-147 Cheapside, London, E.C.2

Ford Anglia 105E

In 1959, the old sidevalve Anglia was replaced by a more modern product, well known for the controversial reverse-slope rear window which was supposed to eliminate condensation and increase headroom, while also (surprise!) being cheap to manufacture. Note the increasing emphasis on the enjoyment of motoring for its own sake, and compare this piece with its 1953 equivalent – some change.

The car
the world has chosen
for its own

"Minx FOR RELIABILITY"

—SAYS EIRE

"Smooth running, perfect balance, exceptional comfort, and power and reliability under all tests!"
Hugh P. O'Neill, Eire.

"Minx FOR ECONOMY"

—SAYS HOLLAND

"Four of us—with luggage—went over the Simplon and St. Gothard 'cols' at 31 miles to the gallon!"
H. F. A. Margadant, Amsterdam.

"Minx FOR PERFORMANCE"

—SAYS SWITZERLAND

"Our good and faithful Minx performs beautifully and climbs hills like mad!" *A. Fischer, Zurich.*

You get so much more in the

Hillman
Minx

and you get so much more out of it

A PRODUCT OF THE ROOTES GROUP

HILLMAN MOTOR CAR CO. LTD. COVENTRY   LONDON SHOWROOMS AND EXPORT DIVISION : ROOTES LTD. DEVONSHIRE HOUSE PICCADILLY LONDON W.I

Hillman Minx Phase V

The testimonial approach is used to endorse the postwar saloon, here portrayed with surprising accuracy. The plaudits also served to irritate the car starved home market, which wanted this no doubt delightful car but was unable to get it. Introduced in 1948, the Minx enjoyed a run of almost ten years, providing that "little bit extra" to economical motorists. Fuel consumption running fast would be surprisingly high, however, and the steering column gearchange was something of an acquired taste.

Be first with the last word!

Hillman
Californian

£510 plus P.T. £213.12.6

Style-setter for the future...can be yours

Looked at, or looked out of, the view is superb. Its beautiful lines and dual-colour scheme
are only the beginning. Built into this exciting car are all the qualities that have made
Hillman famous throughout the world . . . performance, safety, and comfort.
Yes, it's the last word in looks . . . the last word, too, in big-car luxury at light-car cost.

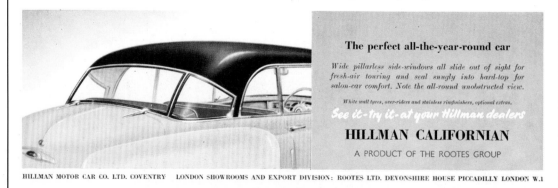

The perfect all-the-year-round car

*Wide pillarless side-windows all slide out of sight for
fresh-air touring and seal snugly into hard-top for
salon-car comfort. Note the all-round unobstructed view.*

White wall tyres, over-riders and stainless rimfinishers, optional extras.

See it-Try it-at your Hillman dealers

HILLMAN CALIFORNIAN

A PRODUCT OF THE ROOTES GROUP

HILLMAN MOTOR CAR CO. LTD. COVENTRY   LONDON SHOWROOMS AND EXPORT DIVISION: ROOTES LTD. DEVONSHIRE HOUSE PICCADILLY LONDON W.1

Hillman Californian

*A typically colourful offering from Rootes, whose advertisements were among the most attractive of the
period. The Californian was an interesting case of an American theme shrunken to British proportions. The
result was dumpier than these illustrations suggest, but the concoction was not without charm, and
demonstrated Rootes' mastery at conjuring style and individuality from relatively modest tooling.*

High jinks?

A day on the links?

A trip to the sphinx?

Every day in every way

you'll be happier in a

Happier with the flashaway zest, the silk-smooth 75 m.p.h.
of the brilliant O.H.V. engine . . .
Happier with its sleek trim luxury look, the roomy, inviting
interior, the big deep boot . . .
Happier with its surefooted grip of the road, its precise
nonsway cornering, its added safety . . .
Happier too, to know that for all its big-car luxury, it costs
as little as ever to run.

Hillman

Minx o.h.v. Convertible
£520 (plus p.t. £217 15 10)
White-wall tyres, over-riders and chromium rimfinishers available as extras

Hillman Minx O.H.V. De Luxe Saloon · Hillman O.H.V. Californian
Hillman Minx Special Saloon · Hillman Estate Car · Hillman Husky

HILLMAN MOTOR CAR CO LTD · COVENTRY · LONDON SHOWROOMS & EXPORT DIVISION: ROOTES LTD · DEVONSHIRE HOUSE · PICCADILLY W.1

Hillman Minx Phase VIII convertible

*Grille modifications indicate the latest version of the Minx. The script is a trifle corny, but the piece has a
certain period appeal. Neglected examples could rattle and shake as badly as most early unitary
convertibles. This one does not have a steering wheel, which enables the same painting to be used in
home and export market advertising – an American pamphlet used the same picture!*

NEW *Double Duty* HILLMAN
at a low price

Comfort and grace...Estate car space

-and 40 m.p.g!

By day the versatile new Hillman Husky is a sturdy 5 cwt. load-carrier. In the evening it's a smart 4-seater family saloon! Comfortable rear seats, neatly folded into the floor, are responsible for this transformation. The Husky has a virile engine that easily meets the Hillman standards of reliability. Design is practical and handsome. Price is low, running cost economical, and at 40 m.p.g. under a wide variation of speed, load and road conditions the Husky is a brilliant answer to more than one motoring problem. Here is the ideal way of serving your business and pleasing the family! Ask your dealer for a free trial NOW.

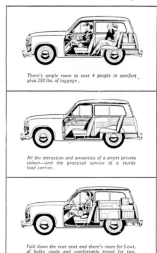

There's ample room to seat 4 people in comfort, plus 250 lbs. of luggage.

All the attraction and amenities of a smart private saloon—and the practical service of a sturdy load carrier.

Fold down the rear seat and there's room for 5 cwt. of bulky goods and comfortable travel for two.

A PRODUCT OF THE ROOTES GROUP

£398
Plus P.T. £166.19.2
White-wall tyres, over-riders and stainless rim nishers available as extras

The *Hillman Husky*
DOUBLES BUSINESS AND PLEASURE

HILLMAN MOTOR CAR CO. LTD. COVENTRY   LONDON SHOWROOMS & EXPORT DIVISION : ROOTES LTD. DEVONSHIRE HOUSE, PICCADILLY, W.1

Hillman Husky

A spiritual ancestor of the hatchback, the Husky was firmly rooted in tradesman's England. The car was slow, noisy and pitched, but it did look almost like a car rather than a light van. There was a van, called the Commer Cob, which looked much the same, give or take some side windows.

The HUMBER Super Snipe

Craftsman Built

BY THE ROOTES GROUP

Wherever in the world your journey takes you, you'll be ahead in the Super Snipe. For here are power and six-seater comfort brilliantly combined. Surging acceleration, 5 - 80 m.p.h. in top gear, with suspension that smoothes out the roughest roads.

Craftsman Serviced

BY YOUR HUMBER DEALER

The craftsmanship of the Super Snipe deserves the craftsman-service that only your Humber Dealer is equipped to provide.

Factory trained mechanics

Specialised tools and equipment · Manufacturers' genuine parts

Guaranteed factory rebuilt units

BY APPOINTMENT   TO H.M. THE KING
MOTOR CAR MANUFACTURERS   HUMBER LIMITED COVENTRY

HUMBER

Humber Ltd Coventry   London Showrooms and Export Division:

ROOTES LTD DEVONSHIRE HOUSE PICCADILLY WI

Humber Super Snipe

The export trade takes priority in 1952 as Super Snipes traverse the continents. The copy is modest, but the artwork superb. The styling of the car is essentially pre-war American, mitigated by a semi-traditional grille and a lack of superfluous decoration. The interior was a combination of traditional and brown-plastic-modern, complete with column change. These cars, with trusty sidevalve engines, lasted well, but looked old-fashioned, and so would be replaced later in the year.

HUMBER PULLMAN LIMOUSINE

Craftsman Built

by

THE ROOTES GROUP

Men of affairs find in the Humber Pullman Limousine —with its 8-seater roominess and exceptional comfort, its grace and dignity, and its powerful performance—all the motoring qualities their position in life demands. And for the owner who on occasions prefers to drive, there is the Imperial Saloon, without dividing partition.

To safeguard the fine qualities of your Humber Pullman, utilize the *specialised* service that only your Humber dealer is equipped to provide:

Craftsman Serviced

by your Humber dealer

- Factory trained mechanics
- Specialised tools and equipment

- Manufacturers' genuine parts
- Guaranteed factory rebuilt units

HUMBER
HAWK · SUPER SNIPE · PULLMAN · IMPERIAL

LONDON SHOWROOMS & EXPORT DIVISION: ROOTES LIMITED · DEVONSHIRE HOUSE · PICCADILLY · LONDON W.1

Humber Pullman

Rearward opening doors distinguish the long wheelbase Pullman and Imperial limousines. The setting is suitably elevated in this April 1952 depiction. There is no need here for the artist to lengthen the car, although a little careful "streamlining" has been employed.

Handsome is –

Styled for the future, elegant and big, the 6-seater Humber Hawk is a car with a fine presence. Cushioned suspension, six smart colour schemes to choose from, and a host of luxury details—proud man, you and your Hawk will go far together!

and Handsome does

The virile, low-revving engine has a capacity *all* of 2267 c.c. Here is smooth power, giving good traffic getaway and high-speed cruising. Large-area brake surfaces and perfect road balance make fast travel safe and comfortable. And the long Humber pedigree is your guarantee of economical, trouble-free motoring.

Ample space here for all the family luggage

£695

PLUS PURCHASE TAX £295.14.2

WHITE-WALL TYRES & CHROMIUM RIMFINISHERS, OPTIONAL EXTRAS

You'll feel great at the wheel of the Hawk

The handsome

By Appointment to the late King George VI Motor Car Manufacturers Humber Ltd.

HUMBER HAWK

A PRODUCT OF THE ROOTES GROUP

HUMBER LIMITED, COVENTRY.   LONDON SHOWROOMS & EXPORT DIVISION: ROOTES LIMITED, DEVONSHIRE HOUSE, PICCADILLY, LONDON, W.I

Humber Hawk Mk V

The new generation of Humbers was represented in 1953 by the Hawk, which had been steadily improved since its introduction in 1948. Gone is the restraint of earlier copy, as an exclamation mark appears beside a gushing text which massacres a smug little proverb that is bad enough in original form! Fortunately for Humber, the car was not nearly as bad as the copy. The use of several blocks of type with small paintings is typical of British advertisements of the period, though the Americans (who favoured such an approach before the war) had largely deserted such layouts. Britain would soon follow.

NEW HUMBER HAWK

ESTATE CAR

6 seater luxury and **exceptional capacity**

*By Appointment
to the late King George VI
Motor Car Manufacturers
Humber Ltd.*

HUMBER

FOR THE FIRST TIME—a big, *luxury* estate car at a reasonable cost!
6 seater saloon comfort, ample loading space and the smartest lines
you've ever seen on an estate car! Powered by the famous
O.H.V. Hawk engine, it has the same excellent suspension and safety
chassis. OVERDRIVE (available as an extra) means even better
performance and even less petrol consumption
(especially in the country!). See your dealer to-day.

£885 plus p.t.

White-wall tyres & chromium rimfinishers available as extras.
A ROOTES PRODUCT

HUMBER LIMITED · COVENTRY · LONDON SHOWROOMS AND EXPORT DIVISION: ROOTES LIMITED · DEVONSHIRE HOUSE · PICCADILLY, W.I

Humber Hawk Mk VI Estate Car

An estate version of the Hawk was a 1955 débutante, and gave Rootes a car to which there was no direct rival from elsewhere. The Ford was less attractive, and there was as yet no Vauxhall estate at all, apart from the occasional one-off. This car falls very much into the American mould, with a roll-up tailgate window to go with the bench seats and, of course, the column-change. The contemporary Hillman Estate Car (with van-type doors at the back) looked downright crude by comparison.

The famous 3½-litre 'D' TYPE JAGUAR with disc brakes, now joins the Jaguar range

The JAGUAR
Range of Models for 1955

THE MARK VII 3½-LITRE SALOON (*Type 'M'*)

In the 1955 range of models Jaguar present not only added refinements but mechanical advances directly derived from unrivalled international experience in racing, record-breaking and endurance tests.

The elegant lines of the Mark VII remain unchanged but the famous XK engine now with high-lift cams has power output raised to 190 b.h.p. Increased diameter torsion bars give even greater riding comfort. New close-ratio gears increase performance in indirect ranges. New 'wrap-around' bumpers afford extra protection. Flasher type indicators, individually adjustable fog lamps and rear lights incorporating reflectors are among new features.

Sports models for 1955 include the famous Jaguar " D " type with disc brakes and dry sump lubrication. The XK 140 Fixed-Head close coupled 2-3 seater, the XK 140 Drop-Head 2-seater and the XK 140 Open 2-seater are powered by the XK 3½-litre engine now with high-lift cams—developing 190 b.h.p. (*Special equipment models are fitted with " C " type engines, wire wheels and fog lamps.*) New features include:—Rack and pinion steering; close-ratio gears for higher performance in indirect ranges; robust 'wrap-around' bumpers; re-designed radiator grille etc.

XK 140 FIXED-HEAD 2-3 SEATER

XK 140 OPEN 2-SEATER

**STAND 129
EARLS COURT**

XK 140 DROP-HEAD 2-SEATER COUPE

Jaguar range for 1955

The Jaguar range at Motor Show time, 1954. All the cars were excellent value, and were in demand abroad as well as at home. The Mk VII saloon, which had been in production since 1951, was given minor modifications. C and D-type Jaguars were very successful in competition during the fifties, which lent prestige to the production cars.

JAGUAR

PRESENTS THE

Two-point-four LITRE

To the already famous range of Jaguars exemplified by the Mark VII and XK140 models, comes the 2.4 litre Jaguar saloon, a brilliant newcomer in which will be found the embodiment of all the highly specialised technical knowledge and engineering achievement that have gained for the name of Jaguar the highest international repute. For over four years Jaguar engineers and technicians have worked to produce, not simply a new model, but an entirely new car of such outstanding merit as to be worthy of presentation to a world which has for long been accustomed to expect great things from Jaguar. How well they have succeeded is made manifest by the specification and performance of the 2.4 litre, a car which derives its character and breeding from every reward of Jaguar endeavour, every phase of Jaguar achievement and every lesson learned in the hard school of international racing. In its outward appearance, the unmistakable Jaguar line of grace is seen with lesser, more compact overall dimensions than those of the Mark VII, yet the interior has been so skilfully planned that full accommodation for five persons is provided and further provision made for generous luggage accommodation. As its name implies, the "Two-point-Four" is powered by an engine of 2.4 litres capacity and is the latest development of the famous six-cylinder, double overhead camshaft, twin carburetter XK engine which, in engineering circles throughout the world, is acclaimed as the most advanced high efficiency production engine in existence. With a power output of 112 brake horsepower and a power/weight ratio of 90 brake horsepower per ton, phenomenal acceleration is placed at the driver's command and, if desired, a maximum speed of over 100 m.p.h. reached with the ease, silence and refinement which are amongst the inimitable characteristics of every Jaguar. Allied to these characteristics are superb road-holding and braking qualities inseparable from all Jaguar cars. To those motorists whose desire for a car of compact dimensions is a matter of personal preference the opportunity is at last presented, not only for satisfying that desire, but for gratifying a natural wish to own a car, the mere possession of which indicates insistence on owning nothing but the best . . . . . a Jaguar.

PRICES : STANDARD MODEL £895 *(with purchase tax £1,269.0.10.)*
SPECIAL EQUIPMENT MODEL £916 *(with purchase tax £1,298.15.10.)*

STAND 154 EARLS COURT

. . . a new Jaguar masterpiece

Jaguar 2.4 saloon

The text of this advertisement for the new "compact" Jaguar is interesting for its explanatory, rather than hectoring, approach. The copy attempts to be measured and aristocratic, but is not without flaw, suggesting a copywriter who is trying to emulate a style not his own. Ironically, some traditionalists of the time accused the Jaguar of possessing only ersatz breeding, but those for whom such considerations were less important than good performance and comfort found a very satisfying car. Much attention was paid to small details, including the sound of the doors closing, for which wood was deemed essential. Very few of this, the standard model, were made.

Same Stable

BRADFORD

JAVELIN

JUPITER

The Javelin now has the new Series III engine which retains the Javelin's well proved horizontally opposed principle but incorporates the modifications resulting from five years of successful international competition work and strenuous overseas use. The

The new Jupiter luggage boot

Jupiter also has the Series III engine tuned for specially high performance —and behind the driver is a roomy tonneau and luggage boot. The Bradford

Commercial range—van, utility, and lorry, is known all over the world for its amazing economy and sturdy reliability. These three cars come from the same famous Yorkshire stable of Jowett Cars Limited who have been making cars for nearly half a century.

JOWETT
of BRADFORD

JOWETT CARS LIMITED, IDLE, BRADFORD AND 48 ALBEMARLE STREET, PICCADILLY, LONDON, W.I.

Jowett range, 1952

Swansong of a much-loved make. While the Jupiter had some success in competition, and the Javelin was well regarded by those who took the trouble to look after it properly, neither car was reliable enough when subjected to long-term abuse to sell as well as had been hoped. The Bradford van, a pre-war hangover with prodigious climbing ability, survived into 1953, and its archaic looks mattered not at all. It did matter that Briggs, who supplied Javelin bodies, were controlled by Ford. A combination of factors therefore led to the demise of the make in 1954.

Taking the rough — *smo-o-o-othly!*

What joy to drive in the Lanchester! Silken-smooth gear change, light yet commanding steering and wonderful road holding stability under all conditions. New laminated-torsion-bar suspension and telescopic shock absorbers smooth out cobblestones, pavé or potholes. There's plenty of room for 5 passengers to relax and stretch their legs in really 'big car' comfort!

'Handsome is as handsome does' goes the old saying— and, judged by these standards, the Lanchester is a very handsome car indeed. The good looks of its swift modern styling are there for all the world to see—but added to these is rugged, sturdy construction, only fully appreciated when you start to take the rough with the smooth. Then you will revel in the superb suspension which takes the kick out of the worst roads; then you will enjoy the way it holds the road, its effortless high speed cruising and the cushioned drive of its fluid transmission*.

*Licensed under Vulcan-Sinclair & Daimler Patents.

the lively, likeable Lanchester

BY APPOINTMENT
Motor Car Manufacturers
To the late King George VI

THE LANCHESTER MOTOR CO. LTD. COVENTRY

 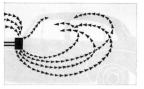

Above left: *Cutaway picture of the actual fluid flywheel. In this transmission there is no rigid mechanical connection; a fluid cushioning effect between engine and roadwheels gives utmost smoothness of drive and gear change.* **Above right:** *Fresh air conditioning with built in heater and ventilating fan. Fresh air circulated, heated or unheated. Control from dash.*

Lanchester Fourteen

An attractive painting announces the Lanchester for 1952. The copy is typical of the period, but that silly, affectedly virtuous little proverb, also favoured by Humber, makes its appearance in what is otherwise a modest script. The Lanchester was, effectively, a smaller-engined and slightly less well equipped Daimler Conquest, and it did not sell in large numbers. It was well-regarded, and a version with steel body framing was exported. Export advertising used similar illustrations, reversing the interior depiction in order to give lefthand-drive! The semi-technical diagrams are typical early fifties, as are the passengers' clothes.

Land-Rover

A mid-fifties advertisement for the Land-Rover. It was intended as a stopgap model, but was so much in demand that production continued for decades. The inspiration is clearly Jeep. This piece is interesting for a complete absence of text, and for the illustration which, unlike many paintings for advertisements, does not attempt to give the appearance of a photograph.

a lovely car

from every angle

"The simple elegance of her line is just perfect."

" Such a luxurious interior is rare these days—"

" Performance gets top marks from me."

Everyone's pleased with the M.G. Magnette! It combines the spirited performance of a true sporting thoroughbred with the elegance and comfort of a luxury saloon. Facia panel and interior woodwork are of solid walnut. Deep, comfortable seating is upholstered in real leather. Carpeting is sumptuous. And with all this luxury goes a liveliness of acceleration that is quite exceptional. At cruising speeds the inimitable Magnette grips the road tightly —rides smoothly, silently and safely. Ask your M.G. dealer for a demonstration.

REMEMBER
Quality and dependability are guaranteed by the B.M.C. Used-Car Warranty and you are certain of a good deal when you sell.

MG 1½ **LITRE MAGNETTE**

Safety fast !

THE M.G. CAR COMPANY LIMITED, SALES DIVISION, COWLEY, OXFORD

London Showrooms: Stratton House, 80 Piccadilly, London, W.1
Overseas Business: Nuffield Exports Limited, Cowley, Oxford, and 41 Piccadilly, London, W.1

MG Magnette ZA

The shape was modern, along the lines of the Wolseley 4/44 in conjunction with which it was designed by Gerald Palmer. The Magnette was spared the Wolseley's column shift, however, and was fitted with a luxurious interior of good quality. The Magnette was a sporting car, with excellent handling, and while the comments here are stilted to modern eyes, they were largely justified. Survivors are much sought after.

1st of a new line

TO MEET THE CHALLENGE OF TOMORROW ON ROAD & TRACK

THE COMPLETELY NEW

MG SERIES
MGA

£595 . 0 . 0 *Ex Works plus*
£249 . 0 . 10 *Purchase Tax*

This potential trophy-winner breaks clean away from traditional M.G. styling, yet inherits all the qualities and fine craftsmanship that have for over a quarter of a century distinguished its famous predecessors. Many of its features are identical to those embodied and tested in George Eyston's record-smashing M.G. Special. Faster...sturdier...safer, it holds the road like a limpet and its 1500 cc. o.h.v. engine puts up a performance that is quite exceptional.

Safety fast

PROFILED FOR PERFORMANCE

THE M.G. CAR COMPANY LIMITED, SALES DIVISION, COWLEY, OXFORD
London Showrooms: Stratton House, 80 Piccadilly, London, W.1
Overseas Business: Nuffield Exports Limited, Cowley, Oxford, and 41 Piccadilly, London, W.1

MG A Sports

Naughty! Read carefully, as it hasn't won yet, being only a "potential trophy winner". This is the first series of MG A, introduced in 1955 to replace the pretty, but antediluvian TF. It looks neat, and vaguely XK Jaguar/BMW inspired. The whitewalls would be preferred by Americans, who would get most of the cars produced. It no doubt reassured British enthusiasts to see the car in right hand drive form here. It sold almost 60,000 by the time it was upgraded in 1959.

In a class of its own for "Quality First" Features

The "*Quality First*"

MORRIS

Take a searching look at the next modern Morris you see. In its styling, interior appointments, superfine finish and in its performance too, it has entered a new and higher class in economical motoring. Until that happy day comes when you take delivery of a new Morris keep your present model in first-class condition by having it serviced regularly by your Morris dealer. There are over 2,000 authorised dealers throughout Britain who are specialists in Morris methods and carry stocks of factory-inspected spares.

 MORRIS MOTORS LIMITED, COWLEY, OXFORD. OVERSEAS BUSINESS: NUFFIELD EXPORTS LIMITED, OXFORD, AND 41 PICCADILLY, LONDON, W.1
C.C.608.

THE FIELD, with which is incorporated *Land and Water* and *The County Gentleman*, is published every Friday, price 1/6, by THE HARMSWORTH PRESS LTD., 8, Stratton Street, London, W.1. Saturday, December 22, 1951. Printed by SIR JOSEPH CAUSTON & SONS, LTD., 72, Fleet Street, London, E.C.4, and Eastleigh, Hants. PRINTED IN GREAT BRITAIN and entered as second class matter at the Post Office, New York, N.Y., March, 1897.

Morris Oxford MO

This advertisement for the sidevalve Oxford makes explicit what everyone knew – that there was little chance in 1951 of getting such a car. While demonstrating that the new model is worth waiting for, it was necessary for the makers to ensure that potential buyers with Morris cars did not give up and put their names down for Hillmans or Austins instead. And the dealers and service agents still needed work, so rigorous servicing of obsolete models was encouraged.

It's a shocking business
Testing Springs!

We start off by choosing a pot-hole in a road. Our engineers take a stony-hearted joy in picking out really spiteful ones, the ideal pot-hole being the sort that makes a motorist's vertebrae sound like a game of dice. Then we take an actual cast of the pot-hole in plaster. When this gets to the works we make a metal copy of it to fit the revolving drums of the pot-hole machine. Now we can get to business!

Any one out of hundreds of Nuffield vehicles on the production line is liable to be kidnapped and "taken for a ride" on the tester, as our large illustration shows. Into a couple of days are packed all the jolts, jars and shocks that a car is likely to meet in five years' driving. If its suspension can stand that, it can stand anything short of going over a precipice.

And the reason for all this? It is just another test to ensure that quality is never left to chance, to ensure that Nuffield products can compete in the markets of the world. And compete they do! Last year Nuffield exported a record total of 103,208 vehicles, worth approximately £36½ million! Which is, of course, another good reason for collecting malicious-looking pot-holes!

Nothing is ever left to chance - by

NUFFIELD ORGANIZATION

MORRIS · WOLSELEY · RILEY · MG · MORRIS-COMMERCIAL VEHICLES · NUFFIELD UNIVERSAL TRACTORS
S.U. CARBURETTERS · MORRIS MARINE ENGINES

Overseas business: Nuffield Exports Limited, Cowley, Oxford, and at 41 Piccadilly, London, W.I.

Morris Oxford (Nuffield)

Endurance tests were a popular Nuffield advertising theme in 1952, just prior to the firm's merger with Austin to form BMC. This is one of a short series. The suspension of the Oxford gave good handling, but if the linkage was at all worn, the car could be jolted badly by potholes, giving rise to much noise if rarely any damage. The inspector, to the right of the picture, looks as if he himself has been struck on the rump, and is suffering in sympathy!

Morris Minor MM

Enlightening a new generation of potential car buyers in 1952. The target market is the middle-class couple, and the inclusion of an extra couple is an assurance not only of four-seater accommodation, but of social acceptability. The elongator has been at work, and the man in the back seat would have to take his golf clubs inside the car, as they would not fit in the boot with all the other luggage. No wonder the dog looks so uncomfortable!

MORRIS OXFORD SALOON
£525 (plus £219.17.6 P.T.)

Thinking of buying a new car? Then let "Pounds, Shillings and Sense" be the deciding factor. Consider initial cost in relation to performance and comfort, and, above all, its ultimate value as a "trade-in" proposition. Away ahead of cars bought on this sensible and calculated basis is the "Quality First" Morris. Any car chosen from the Morris range is unsurpassed for its responsive acceleration and high cruising average . . . its craftsmanship, finish, comfort and styling . . . and its perpetuation of pride in ownership. When the time comes to change you'll realise how well the "Quality First" Morris has maintained its value.

It pays to buy a

SERVICE IN EUROPE: Morris owners planning a Continental Tour are invited to see their Morris dealer for details of a free service to save foreign currency.

REMEMBER:— *Quality and dependability are guaranteed by the B.M.C. Used-Car Warranty and you are certain of a good deal when you sell.*

MORRIS MOTORS LTD., COWLEY, OXFORD. London Distributors: Morris House, Berkeley Square, London, W.1. Overseas Business: Nuffield Exports Limited, Oxford & 41 Piccadilly, London, W.1.

C.220(55)

72

Morris Oxford Series II

The mainstream middle-market car is proposed with a twee little pun. The car was much livelier, and usefully more spacious than its predecessor, and enjoyed a good following. Morris deliberately allied themselves with middle-class family values of thrift, value for money over the long term and quality – hence the "Quality First" slogan, and a reluctance to omit the couple or family from illustrations. From time to time this targeting gave rise to some very silly copy "gilt-edged security for one's satisfaction" and "the amenities of lounge-easy travel" were other favoured phrases on which even Morris owners must have choked.

Happiest Return
in motoring!

The New "QUALITY FIRST"
MORRIS Cowley

Even the seasoned motorist, recalling with affection the 'Cowley' of other days, will marvel at the value offered by this latest Morris Cowley — new and Quality First. The new Cowley is destined to be just as popular as the Morris Minor, in a higher horse-power class.

Here, brighter than ever, is the Cowley tradition—honest quality and reliability in a really economical family car. For a new generation of motorists, these rewarding virtues are combined with the high cruising speed and fast get-away of a powerful O.H.V. engine, beautiful modern styling, a roomy, well-appointed interior, and many other Quality First features.

The Pick of the Points

- High-performance 1200 c.c. O.H.V. Engine
- Controllable air intake and provision for heater
- Safety Glass throughout
- Independent Front Wheel suspension
- Deep, multi-coat finish in enduring colours
- Widest seating width ever
- Hydraulically actuated clutch
- 16 cu. ft. luggage space
- Full width rear window
- Twin self-parking windscreen wipers
- Pull-up hand brake lever at side of seat

"Quality First" means Value-First throughout the Morris Range

- SERVICE IN EUROPE: Morris owners planning a Continental Tour are invited to see their Morris dealer for details of a free service to save foreign currency.

MORRIS MOTORS LIMITED, COWLEY, OXFORD.
London Distributors: Morris House, Berkeley Square, W.1. Overseas Business: Nuffield Exports Limited, Oxford & 41 Piccadilly, London, W.1.

C. 189A (54)

Morris Cowley

In 1954, the new Oxford was joined by the new Cowley, a gutless Austin-engined utility Oxford which never sold in anything like the large numbers of its better equipped sibling. The Cowley was economical driven gently, but the good caning it needed to build up respectable speed reduced the margin considerably. This Cowley looks rather doleful, as if prescient of poor sales, and the painting does not really do justice to its trim lines. Note the BMC rosette which replaced the Nuffied symbol on Morris advertisements, following the 1952 merger with Austin.

One test drive...

will tell you more than

For accent on high performance in a more spacious luxury car, meet the "Isis"—the biggest Morris in Morris history! Its 2639 c.c. six-cylinder overhead-valve engine packs a power-punch to give phenomenal acceleration, high cruising speed and road supremacy under all conditions. Take it for a trial drive—its performance will do the talking!

a thousand words

I'm going to have a

"QUALITY FIRST"
MORRIS

MINOR · COWLEY · OXFORD · ISIS

REMEMBER
Quality and dependability are guaranteed by the B.M.C. Used-Car Warranty and you are certain of a good deal when you sell.

MORRIS MOTORS LTD., COWLEY, OXFORD.   London Distributors: Morris House, Berkeley Sq., W.1.
Overseas Business: Nuffield Exports Ltd., Oxford & 41 Piccadilly, London, W.1.

Morris Isis

The name was a pre-war revival, and the Isis was, effectively, a six-cylinder version of the contemporary Oxford. The 2.6-litre engine, shared with several other BMC cars, was powerful and reliable, but the handling precision of the smaller car was lost. Objectively speaking, the Isis was not a success, and it was Austin's rival Westminster that would get the "Farina" treatment in a few years, while the Morris faded from view.

Together...

and enjoying life in a

"QUALITY FIRST"

MORRIS

The moment 'Minor' owners meet there's a mutual admiration society in session—with the Minor 1000 as the star! And always on the agenda are compliments to the sparkling power, comfort and economy of this classic car.

There's room for another elbow on the bonnet! Why not join in! It feels good to be a Minor owner. The world's happiest motorists are carried unanimously . . . in the Minor 1000.

World famous 948 c.c. OHV engine / full 4-seater inter-axle comfort / superb suspension and road-holding / rack and pinion steering / safety door locks / big-car features and amenities . . . and, in everything, Morris Quality First.

Twelve Months' Warranty and backed by B.M.C. Service—the most comprehensive in Europe.

MORRIS MINOR 1000. Prices from £416 (plus £174.9.2 P.T.)
MORRIS MINI-MINOR. Prices from £350 (plus £146.19.2 P.T.)
MORRIS OXFORD. Prices from £575 (plus £240.14.2 P.T.)

MORRIS MOTORS LTD., COWLEY, OXFORD. *London Distributors: Morris House Berkeley Square, London, W.1. Overseas Business: NUFFIELD EXPORTS LTD., OXFORD, and at 41-46 Piccadilly, London, W.1*
922/A

Morris Minor 1000

The "togetherness" theme in Morris advertising persisted for some years; this 1959 incarnation of the Morris Minor is depicted as a social lubricant, a role it continued to fulfil even into the 1980s, when owners would wave at each other as they passed on the road. Some aspects of this four-door Deluxe were crude by 1959, such as the dozens of exposed screw heads inside the car, the semaphore indicators, and the considerable noise. But the Minor was of essentially good quality, and prodigiously reliable unless completely neglected. It largely sold itself until finally going out of production in 1971.

Together...

and enjoying life in a

"QUALITY FIRST"

MORRIS
OXFORD

Twelve Months' Warranty and backed by B.M.C. Service — the most comprehensive in Europe.

MORRIS OXFORD. Prices from £575 (plus £240.14.2 Purchase Tax)
MORRIS MINOR 1000. Prices from £416 (plus £174.0.2 Purchase Tax)
MORRIS MINI-MINOR. Prices from £350 (plus £146.19.2 Purchase Tax)

MORRIS MOTORS LTD., COWLEY, OXFORD.
London Distributors: Morris House, Berkeley Square, W.1. Overseas Business: Nuffield Exports Ltd., Oxford and at 41-46 Piccadilly, London, W.1.

Saturday shopping in a jam-packed market town. Not everyone's idea of heaven! But *we* look at life through the windows of an Oxford. And somehow an Oxford makes everything fun. It's a dream car to drive. A dream to look at. Equally comfortable for front *and* back seat drivers. Masses of room in the luggage trunk. Exceptional . . . but, listen— there's so much to tell, why not try out an Oxford and see for yourself?

Long low lines / gay colours and duotones / 1500 c.c. OHV engine / over 70 m.p.h. and up to 35 m.p.g. / panoramic vision / child-proof locks / safety steering wheel / Morris "Quality First" all through.

Morris Oxford Series V

The Morris version of BMC's Pininfarina styled 1½-litre range was just a little more upmarket than the Cambridge. The "togetherness" theme remains, but the script is gushing and exclamatory. The new Oxford was a rugged car, and could put up with much abuse. The description of the boot as a trunk, à l'Americaine, is surprising.

THE FIELD, November 23 1961

OPEN ON CHRISTMAS DAY

This is a moment of magic.
The smell of polished leathercloth.
The rich, gleaming finish.
A new car to explore – a new life
to enjoy. A new Morris! The fabulous
'Mini-Minor' has slipped into
this Christmas scene. But see the
'Oxford' and 'Minor 1000' as well . . .
all present and Quality First
at your Morris dealer!

We're going to have a
QUALITY FIRST
MORRIS

Morris Mini-Minor.
Also the Morris Oxford and
Morris Minor 1000.
Twelve Months' Warranty and
backed by B.M.C. Service.

Morris Motors Limited,
Cowley, Oxford.
Overseas Business:
Nuffield Exports Limited,
Oxford and at 41-46
Piccadilly, London W.1.

Morris Mini Minor

Judicious badge shuffling has produced a Morris version of the new Mini, photographed in a delightfully ingenuous Christmas setting. The car, originally intended as a working man's economy vehicle, eventually found most favour with those who could afford something bigger if they chose, but who liked the Mini's novelty and convenience. The Mini cult did not take off immediately, but good performance and excellent handling made it much more fun than the larger Ford Popular which, in 1959, could be had for similar money, and at a vastly greater profit for its makers.

Yes indeed! **Riley** for Magnificent Motoring

Performance figures for the Riley 2½ litre are impressive by any standards. They tell a story of flashing acceleration and a maximum of over 100 m.p.h. But they cannot describe the quality of the distinctive, individually built Riley.

They cannot tell you how engine, steering, suspension, brakes and even body, all blend to give Riley character.

Owning and driving a Riley are two of the fine pleasures that words cannot express.

2½ litre Saloon. 1½ litre Saloon.

Riley – as old as the industry – as modern as the hour

RILEY MOTORS LIMITED, Sales Division, COWLEY, OXFORD. London Showrooms: "RILEY CARS," 55-56 Pall Mall, S.W.1
Overseas Business: Nuffield Exports Ltd., Oxford and 41 Piccadilly, London, W.1

Riley RMB 2½ Litre

By 1952, the RM series Rileys had established themselves as excellent family cars for the enthusiast. Built along pre-war lines, the RM had a steel-panelled body on an ash frame, and a distinctive fabric roof. The car was fast – over 90 mph – but heavy to drive, and cornering balance was, if anything, better with the smaller 1½ litre engine. These cars became known as the "last proper Rileys", as after they ceased production, the pre-war breeding would increasingly be diluted by BMC who put Riley grilles on ordinary corporate products.

has something rare to offer . .

Not just a make of car but a tradition of exciting performance and fine workmanship—the idea of a car as an enjoyment rather than merely a means of transport—an engine developed from great race track performers, a delightful quality of steering, sure road-holding, impressively efficient brakes—these are just facets of the Riley character which has made this fine British car one of the most highly regarded by motoring enthusiasts all over the world. Riley ownership is something you go on enjoying.

 *for Magnificent Motoring*

1½ litre Saloon 2½ litre Saloon

RILEY MOTORS LIMITED, *Sales Division*, COWLEY, OXFORD
London Showrooms RILEY CARS, 55-58 PALL MALL, S.W.1   *Overseas Business* Nuffield Exports Ltd., Oxford and 41 Piccadilly, London, W.1

Riley RME 1½ Litre

This Riley was expensive for the performance offered, but the enthusiast found a thoughtful layout, firm, consistent controls and an excellent finish. The steering was precise, and with high gearing that did not pander to the lazy or feeble, but which rewarded the intelligent driver. The driving position derived comfort from position, not padding, and the close-set steering wheel and outstretched, slightly raised leg driving position gave supreme relaxation, which is a revelation to the modern driver who is told the Ergonomics Computer Knows Best, but whose back tells him otherwise.

'THE BEST RILEY YET' vide 'THE MOTOR'

The day you drive your
RILEY PATHFINDER <u>home</u>

Together with his home, nothing is more likely to reflect a man's prestige than the car he prefers to own. It is not surprising therefore that men of discernment to-day aspire to the ownership of the new Riley PATHFINDER. In this car you will discover a rare combination of the luxurious comfort you deserve with the high-speed performance you demand.

You will be impressed by the sweeping grace of its brilliant new styling. At once you will see why it is the car on which so many men have now set their hearts.

But the worth of the PATHFINDER goes deeper—every ounce of skilled Riley engineering experience has been concentrated into this fine car. That is why you can be sure that the PATHFINDER will give you years of thoroughly dependable, trouble-free motoring.

DRIVE THE RILEY PATHFINDER . . . a wonderful experience! In the busiest traffic—so serene!

ON THE OPEN ROAD . . . at more than a mile and a half a minute you are still easy and relaxed.

REMEMBER—
Quality and dependability are guaranteed by the B.M.C. Used-Car Warranty and you are certain of a good deal when you sell.

The Riley Pathfinder is fitted with Safety Glass all round.

 ## FOR MAGNIFICENT MOTORING

RILEY MOTORS LIMITED, Sales Division, COWLEY, OXFORD
London Showrooms: RILEY CARS, 55-56 PALL MALL, S.W.1 Overseas Business: Nuffield Exports Ltd., Oxford and 41 Piccadilly, London, W.1

Riley Pathfinder

The Pathfinder was a copywriter's nightmare. As the corporate accountants decreed an end to the ''pure'' Riley, to the outrage of enthusiasts from pre-war days, the Jaguar 2.4 poached many potential sales to customers who did not object to the inevitable progress. Add to this dilemma a deterioration in handling and reliability, and one can hardly blame the copywriter for trading on the prestige of the Riley name, rather than on the merits of the Pathfinder itself. Treated sensibly, later examples were apparently quite pleasant, but the ''ditchfinder'' nickname, given to early examples, which suffered rear suspension trouble, was the kind of wisecrack that lodged in sceptical minds.

BY APPOINTMENT
TO HER MAJESTY THE QUEEN
COACHBUILDERS & MOTOR BODY BUILDERS
HOOPER & CO (COACHBUILDERS) LTD

BY APPOINTMENT
TO HER MAJESTY QUEEN ELIZABETH THE QUEEN MOTHER
MOTOR BODY BUILDERS
HOOPER & CO (COACHBUILDERS) LTD

HOOPER

*Hooper Touring Limousine Design No 8390
on Rolls-Royce Silver Wraith*

THIS CAR WILL BE SHOWN AT
THE MOTOR SHOW, EARLS COURT
STAND 106, OCT 19 TO OCT 29

HOOPER AND COMPANY (COACHBUILDERS) LIMITED

54 St. James's Street, Piccadilly, London, SW1.   Telephone: Hyde Park 3242

OFFICIAL RETAILERS OF ROLLS ROYCE, DAIMLER AND BENTLEY. DISTRIBUTORS OF LANCHESTER CARS

Rolls-Royce "Hooper" Silver Wraith

Hooper's "Empress Line" style is here fitted to a Silver Wraith chassis. It is an interesting combination of stylistic motifs, using faired-in front wings and wheel spats, for which the Americans were best known, with a Chrysler Airflow Imperial style windscreen, combined with a traditional grille and freestanding headlamps. This is an unusual advertisement; the market for such cars was stable, and clients would not decide to buy as a result of media saturation. The Motor Show was an appropriate time discreetly to remind potential clients of what was available.

ROLLS-ROYCE
The Best Car in the World

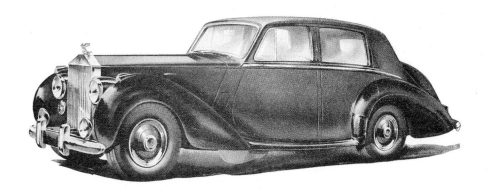

THE SILVER DAWN

An Owner-Driver Saloon

with coachwork by Rolls-Royce and available with

the automatic gearbox.

Rolls-Royce Silver Dawn

The Dawn was a well-proportioned car, and many coachbuilders' efforts were not as pleasing as this Standard Steel body. Rust would become a problem in neglected examples. This advertisement typifies the maker's well-known laconic approach to copy.

The Best Car in the World

Whatever the weather—full ventilation, air conditioning or heating ensure a journey in complete comfort for driver and passengers of the Rolls-Royce Silver Cloud II.

The powerful 8-cylinder aluminium engine gives acceleration and performance in excess of any previous Rolls-Royce. This, together with fully automatic transmission and power-assisted steering makes it possible to maintain high average speeds without fatigue. An exceptionally high degree of safety is provided by three separate braking systems —two hydraulic and one mechanical, acting independently and in concert.

By Appointment to
Her Majesty The Queen
Motor Car Manufacturers
Rolls-Royce Limited

Rolls-Royce Silver Cloud

A V8 engine succeeded the earlier six, and the body, common to both, clothed the last mainstream Royce with a separate chassis. This car appears to be parked with lights out, facing the wrong way up a one-way street, and marks a foray into "atmospheric" portraiture.

The
ROVER
Seventy Five

ONE OF BRITAIN'S FINE CARS

Rover 75

Serenity amidst the storm. This delightful painting dates from 1953, and in its colouring subtly reflects the artistic genre which would most appeal to Rover's intended clientèle. Good taste, restraint and quality were the characteristics for which the Rover was renowned, but when introduced, this car was controversially nouveau. The exaggerated length of this depiction increases the car's resemblance to the American Studebaker of a few years earlier. This was no accident, as Rover imported at least one such car for evaluation and testing. How many owners knew of the connection?

THE NEW ROVER PROGRAMME

New high performance specification and new power-braking for the 90. Greater comfort in all three models — the 60, 75 and 90.

THE NINETY

HIGH PERFORMANCE By increasing the compression ratio, the acceleration has become still more vivid. An optional overdrive ensures a higher maximum speed, exceptionally fast and silent cruising at low engine speeds and a useful saving in petrol consumption. Top gear flexibility, so valuable when driving in traffic, is unaffected.

EXTRA SAFETY To match this livelier performance, a new Servo-assisted braking system is introduced. This ensures impressive light-pressure stopping from high speeds and maximum safety under modern road conditions.

THE SIXTY, SEVENTY-FIVE AND NINETY

EXTRA COMFORT Rover cars have a fine reputation for driver and passenger comfort. There is now a choice of two styles in the front seating—a bench type seat or, as an optional extra, two individual seats independently adjustable. The deep hide upholstery is pleated to retain its shape and the rear arm rests have been redesigned for greater comfort.

Prices including purchase tax, '60': £1191.2.6; '75': £1297.7.6; '90': £1339.17.6. (overdrive, optional extra)

THE ROVER COMPANY LIMITED · SOLIHULL · BIRMINGHAM also DEVONSHIRE HOUSE · LONDON

Rover 90 Saloon

Trying that little bit harder as the home market warms up in 1955, Rover tell their clients why they should choose the new style saloon. Studebaker had long since moved on to chrome-laden coupes, and detail changes to the body lend the Rover an increasingly conservative British air. The effect is that a car known for its solid quality consolidates its market niche, and the text is hardly hysterical, with not an exclamation mark in sight. The general rule with an upmarket car was persuade your clients by all means, but do not shout at them . . .

Mighty Hunters...

*In Greek Mythology Orion was
a Mighty Hunter; in the constellations
he remains immortalized
amongst the stars*

the bright star
of the motor world to-day is the

HUNTER

THERE IS NO CAR MADE BETTER
YOU WILL APPRECIATE THE FINE QUALITIES OF THE HUNTER
WHEN DEMONSTRATED BY YOUR LOCAL DISTRIBUTOR

PRICE £687·10·0 EX WORKS   *Plus Purchase Tax* £287·11·8

the car that is built on a Chassis

SINGER MOTORS LIMITED
Small Heath · Birmingham . . . also at Coventry

Singer Hunter

A non-sequitur surprising even in an era of quirky copy announces in September 1955 that the Hunter is a well-made car (which it was). This is what the earlier SM 1500 should have been – the new grille arrangement has turned the ugly duckling, if not into a swan, then at least into a passable automotive duck. The interior was improved, with the 1940s American style mock woodgrain dashboard, from the earlier car, retained with better instruments. The engine and chassis were largely 1948. Here the artist at last has a dominant feature to work on, and the copywriter can have fun with a new name. An attractive horse's head mascot was fitted to add distinction.

Eighty Progressive Years...

In the mythology of Ancient Greece the ultimate in power and performance was symbolised by Apollo who daily drove the sun across the sky in a mighty chariot drawn by many horses. We have chosen this symbol to illustrate the shining and unfailing performance of the Hunter, that superbly refined car representing the skill and craftsmanship of eighty progressive years. From the tiniest detail to its outstanding performance this new Hunter offers proof positive . . . . . .

in the long run experience counts

The car built on a chassis, the Hunter has a 4-cylinder 1½ litre twin-overhead-camshaft engine developing 75 b.h.p. to give maximum speeds approaching 90 m.p.h., and effortless cruising at 75 m.p.h. and outstanding acceleration through the gears. This luxurious 5-6 seater car is fitted with special independent front wheel suspension which ensures safe handling at all speeds.

The **HUNTER** 75

THERE IS NO CAR MADE BETTER

PRICE £811.0.0. *Plus P.T. £339.0.10*

SINGER MOTORS LTD
Small Heath · Birmingham · also at Coventry

STAND No. 144
Motor Show · Earls Court

Singer Hunter 75 Saloon

An October 1955 advertisement for the more powerful 75 variant. The assertion that there was "no car made better" was provocative and a little hysterical, and demonstrably untrue. The danger with such slogans is that they can be refuted in one word or less! Interestingly for so traditional a car, the bonnet top and side valances were made from glassfibre, which saved tooling costs, until quality control problems dictated a reversion to steel. Less than 5000 Hunters were made, and only a very few were built to 75 specification, with a 75bhp (as opposed to 50bhp) engine.

A scene in Dalecarlia, Sweden

All that's best from Britain . . .

Land of mountains, pine forests and swirling rivers. . . . this is Sweden. Here live a people old in the art of producing fine precision tools, pottery and architecture. . . . a people forward-looking and eager to enjoy the best. . . . that is why the Standard Vanguard is a big favourite with them. Built by the finest engineering craftsmen, tested under the most arduous conditions it is a car that truly represents ' all that's best from Britain.'

Manufactured by THE STANDARD MOTOR CO. LTD., COVENTRY, ENGLAND.

London : 37, Davies Street, Grosvenor Square, W.1. Telephone : Mayfair 5011

The Standard Vanguard

Standard Vanguard Phase 1A

Frustration turned to pride, with a little help from soothing scenery and a notably realistic portrait for the time. Home market buyers who were not "priority users" had little chance of acquiring a new Vanguard in 1952 without a long wait, but the company name still had to be kept before the public eye. If Britain's reputation was enhanced by the car's strong sales abroad, what did it matter that one was forced to eke out one's petrol ration in a worn out Flying Fourteen?

They're proud of IT!

THE STANDARD TEN Price: £409 (P.T. £171.10.10)
OUTRIGHT WINNER OF THIS YEAR'S R.A.C. RALLY

You cannot *see* IT—yet to have IT makes all the difference in the world. And IT is something you'll discover in every Standard car—that extra quality of craftsmanship and performance that makes a Standard such a cherished possession. The Standard Ten, for instance, with its four large doors, its roominess, its economy—40/50 miles to the gallon—and its lively 948 c.c. engine always ready to meet every need. In fact, the car to do *you* proud, at home or abroad.

Standard Cars

THE STANDARD MOTOR COMPANY, LTD., COVENTRY, ENGLAND
London Showrooms: 15-17 Berkeley Square, W.1. Tel: Grosvenor 8181

STANDARD CARS · TRIUMPH CARS · STANDARD COMMERCIAL VEHICLES · STANDARD DIESEL ENGINES · FERGUSON TRACTORS

Standard Ten

In 1954 a new Eight was joined by the Ten, and this 1954 car is being tended by proud new owners, for whom this was possibly the first car that they had ever owned. The wide rear doors were a useful feature, as was the bootlid which was standard on this model (though not on the early Eight, whose luggage compartment was promoted as dust and water proof!). The washbucket and Hoover are amusing period pieces.

IT makes history!

Those Internationally Tested qualities found in all Standard cars are now presented to you in a NEW Standard model—a car for this day and age, superb in its comfort and up-to-the-minute refinements. IT brilliantly makes motoring history once again!

Fitted with the famous 2-litre engine that has already proved its reliability in hundreds of thousands of Standard-made vehicles since the war, the new Vanguard III brings you such features as automatic entry lights to all doors; front doors that can be locked internally or externally as desired;

roomy, deep cushioned comfort for six; simplified, finger-light controls; perfect vision front and rear through wide glass screens; two tail and stop lamps and reversing light placed so that all are easily seen by following vehicles; handsome, aerodynamic body lines, plus these special safety features: doors hinged to open to the rear; dual purpose switches; electrically operated screen washer and air conditioning to avoid window misting. Dunlop tubeless tyres—putting this fine car magnificently miles ahead. . . .

★ *Overdrive can be fitted on 2nd and 3rd gears as an optional extra.*

—the NEW
Standard Vanguard III

PRICE £599 (P.T. £250.14.2) TOTAL **£849.14.2**

THE STANDARD MOTOR COMPANY LTD., COVENTRY, ENGLAND London Showrooms: 15-17 Berkeley Square, W.1 Tel: Grosvenor 8181

STANDARD CARS · TRIUMPH CARS · STANDARD COMMERCIAL VEHICLES · STANDARD DIESEL ENGINES · FERGUSON TRACTORS

716

Standard Vanguard Phase III

"IT" makes a return, with the Phase III Vanguard, now monocoque with sleeker styling than before. The advertisement is hardly imaginative, and it is surprising that the scriptwriter has to descend to such excruciating details as "two tail and stop lamps" and "doors hinged to the rear". Vanguards had been fitted with both for years, along with most other comparable cars. The screen-washer and heater were not items always found on rivals. The car was not nearly as bad as the dismal copy suggests.

'there's a <u>real</u> V.I.P. car'

THE VANGUARD ESTATE CAR

£1,092.13.4. (inc. P.T.). White-wall tyres extra.

STANDARD · TRIUMPH

STANDARD-TRIUMPH GROUP · COVENTRY   LONDON SHOWROOMS · BERKELEY SQUARE

135

Standard "Vignale" Vanguard Estate Car

Standard here indulge in some wishful thinking. It wasn't a real VIP car, and in old age would often serve as a popular builder's hack, but the Vanguard's use by the armed services lent a certain cachet to what was generally a competent and rugged car. The style was still very 1955, and contemporaries from Ford, Vauxhall, Rootes and BMC were sleeker. As ever, if your product is old-fashioned, suggest that it is distinctive.

I've just had the
drive of my life!

When George offered to run me down for the week-end
and bragged about his time from point A to point B, I
expected a pretty hair-raising journey. That Sunbeam-Talbot
of his really is an amazing car. I don't think I've
ever been driven at such a high average speed
and at the same time felt so very comfortable and very safe.

*Ask your dealer for a trial run today
— it will convince you!*

SUNBEAM-TALBOT

*Awarded the Dewar Trophy presented by the Royal Automobile Club for
the most outstanding engineering and technical achievement during 1952*

A PRODUCT OF THE ROOTES GROUP

SUNBEAM-TALBOT LTD, RYTON-ON-DUNSMORE, COVENTRY • LONDON SHOWROOMS & EXPORT DIV: ROOTES LTD, DEVONSHIRE HOUSE, PICCADILLY, W.1

Sunbeam-Talbot 90 Mk IIA

Modest description did not figure too prominently in Rootes advertisements of the mid-fifties, and while not as brash as the copy for the contemporary Minx, this piece is, for the time, hardly restrained. The conversational approach had the merit of being memorable, but could backfire if potential enthusiasts for the car were dissuaded by a projected image which did not appeal. Like golf, the car was gently sporting, but not above mild spivvery when fitted with whitewalls and wheeltrims to complement the painted dashboard, cream plastic steering wheel and, (horror!) "synchromatic" column change.

4 WINNERS
—at the very first attempt!

The New
SUNBEAM
ALPINE

The Sunbeam Alpine 2-seater won no less than *four* Coupes des Alpes in the perilous and back-breaking 1953 International Alpine Trial. Miss Sheila Van Damm was also awarded the Coupe des Dames, for which no lady has qualified since 1939. This was a triumphant debut, following officially timed tests at over 120 m.p.h. Based on the highly successful Sunbeam-Talbot, this great new car, with its glorious lines, indomitable stamina, and really *terrific* performance, is the biggest motoring sensation for years. Now available on the home market—consult your distributor or dealer today.

Whitewall tyres and over-riders, optional extras

SUNBEAM ALPINE
SUNBEAM-TALBOT
PRODUCTS OF THE ROOTES GROUP

SUNBEAM-TALBOT LTD. COVENTRY   LONDON SHOWROOMS AND EXPORT DIVISION: ROOTES LTD. DEVONSHIRE HOUSE PICCADILLY LONDON W.I

Sunbeam Alpine

The Alpine was intended from its inception to be a glamour model, but it achieved notable success in competition. The large size of the car by comparison with many sports machines is apparent, as are the louvred bonnet and unusual windscreen. Rootes advertisements were often memorable for the sense of style and glamour which they injected into some far from exciting cars. In this case, the car looked impressive in the flesh as well as on paper.

The car that has *everything!*

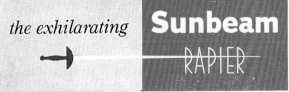
Sunbeam Rapier Series I

The Rapier was a newcomer in 1956, with styling derived from the new Minx. The car looked sporty, but it did not handle well, and the steering column gearchange would soon go. This early Rapier was really the spiritual successor to the Californian, but was equally colourful. This depiction is almost two advertisements in one, as an escapist impression of the car, with no pretension to technical accuracy, is juxtaposed with a prosaic description of boot capacity. Such mixing of approaches was generally avoided.

FOR PEOPLE WITH A zest FOR LIVING

SUNBEAM RAPIER

For people whose life goes with a *zing*, Rootes build the SUNBEAM RAPIER. It has all the pep, power and performance of a sports car, PLUS spacious and luxurious comfort. Styling is rakish and full of character, coach-work and appointments are of a very high standard. A car that's good to look at, good to ride in, pure pleasure to drive. Ask any Rootes Dealer for a free trial run. 1.6 LITRE ENGINE. FRONT DISC BRAKES. WIDE CHOICE OF COLOUR SCHEMES OVERDRIVE ON 3RD AND 4TH GEARS AVAILABLE AT EXTRA COST
SALOON: £705 plus P.T. £324.7.3d. CONVERTIBLE: £745 plus P.T. £342.13.11d
Jack Brabham, World Champion Racing Driver 1959 & 60, knows his cars — and for pleasure, drives a Sunbeam Rapier

BY APPOINTMENT TO HER MAJESTY THE QUEEN
MOTOR VEHICLE MANUFACTURERS
ROOTES MOTORS LIMITED

ROOTES MOTORS LTD

SUNBEAM TALBOT LTD., COVENTRY. LONDON SHOWROOMS AND EXPORT
DIV., ROOTES-MOTORS LTD., DEVONSHIRE HOUSE, PICCADILLY, LONDON, W.1

Sunbeam Rapier Series III

By 1960, the breed had improved, with floor change and a grille which is clearly distinct from that of the Minx. The narrow dark colour flash down the side indicates a post-1959 Series III. Testimonials like this one usually help sales, and Brabham's endorsement would hopefully dispel any reputation for dandyism that persisted from the earlier Rapier and Alpine. Several styling motifs were shared with the American Studebaker Hawk series; this was not a coincidence, as Rootes had consulted the Loewy design studios whose work was crucial to Studebaker.

'IT'S A BEAUT' SAYS JACK BRABHAM

WORLD CHAMPION RACING DRIVER 1959 AND 1960

SUNBEAM ALPINE

now with 1·6 litre engine

'POWER AND GRIP – that's the first impression I had when I tried this great Sunbeam Alpine. Whatever the road was like, you certainly felt that the lively Alpine had things well in hand. This sports car makes you feel good – the road streams away behind you and you know she's got all four corners well down.'

MORE POWER Lively 1592 cc engine develops 85·5 b.h.p., more torque – giving vivid acceleration and ample power.

MORE STABILITY Rear springs are bigger – for greater lateral stability. Larger capacity rear shock absorbers improve ride control and prevent fade.

MORE ROOM There is an extra 1½″ between seat and steering wheel, the pedals are adjustable and the seats move farther back.

MORE REFINEMENTS Better weather sealing . . . detachable hood cant rails . . . an extra interior light . . . eight *less* greasing points . . . quick-action petrol filler cap.

Wire Wheels, White Wall Tyres, Overdrive and Hard-Top are optional extras. You can now choose from *five* colour schemes.

PRICE £695 *plus* P.T. £290.14.2

By Appointment to Her Majesty The Queen
Motor Vehicle Manufacturers
Rootes Motors Limited

ROOTES MOTORS LTD

Sunbeam-Talbot Ltd., Coventry. London Showrooms & Export Div.
Rootes Limited, Devonshire House, Piccadilly, London W.1

Sunbeam Alpine Sports Series II

*The personal testimonial as advertising motif was rare by 1959, though it had been more popular before the war. Being a Rootes product, the car was highly styled, with tailfins, headlamp peaks and a saloon-type steering wheel. Roll-up windows and a well trimmed cabin were features that would become **de rigeur** for sports cars by the middle sixties, sometimes to the chagrin of the hardy souls who considered such things "soft".*

All that's best in Britain...

'He was not for an age, but for all time.' So wrote Ben Jonson of William Shakespeare.

Each year, from the far corners of the earth, men and women come to pay homage to England's greatest poet

at his birthplace. Just as he added lustre to our language, so we today, in our way,

are giving the world new evidence of our genius and our craftsmanship . . . . . . the craftsmanship,

for example, that goes into the products of the Standard Motor Company,

representing as they do in every detail of their design ' all that's best in Britain '.

The 1952 Triumph Renown
SALOON & LIMOUSINE

Manufactured by
THE TRIUMPH MOTOR COMPANY (1945) LTD., COVENTRY
A subsidiary of the Standard Motor Co. Ltd.
London: 37, Davies Street, Grosvenor Square, W.1.
Telephone: MAYfair 5011

TRIUMPH CARS · STANDARD CARS · STANDARD COMMERCIAL VEHICLES · FERGUSON TRACTORS

871

Triumph Renown Saloon

The date is 1951, and Standard-Triumph advertise the Renown with another of the "Best in Britain" series. In the case of this traditionally styled car, the setting is English; in cars intended primarily for export, such as the Vanguard, it would often be foreign. Like Daimler, Triumph pick on a facet of English cultural life, and imply that the production of such a select automobile is a natural continuation of the nation's inventiveness as evinced by Shakespeare, et al. One suspects, however, that there are now more people who recognise the name of Shakespeare than who remember the Renown!

A view of Leblon, a suburb of Rio de Janeiro

All that's best from Britain . . .

Brazil, with its mysterious tropical forests, its great Amazonian waterway, and its beautiful capital city, offers on the one hand the luxury of modern living, and on the other the excitement of the unexplored. For meeting such a variety of conditions its people have found the Triumph Mayflower the ideal car. Built by the finest engineering craftsmen, tested under the most arduous conditions, it truly represents in every detail of its design ' all that's best from Britain.'

The Triumph Motor Co. (1945) Ltd., Coventry, England. A subsidiary of The Standard Motor Co. Ltd.

London: 37, Davies Street, Grosvenor Square, W.1. Telephone: Mayfair 5011

The Triumph Mayflower

Triumph Mayflower

The smaller of the two Triumph "Razor edge" saloons was the Mayflower, whose styling was a controversial reminder of ancient and modern, summed up by motoring enthusiast and rally competitor Helen Marshall as "Queen Anne top and Mary Anne bottom". The little car was well-finished, and was of semi-unitary construction, with a steel body welded to a relatively light chassis frame. The styling remained unimitated, and for the small numbers made, the car is remarkably well remembered, forty years on.

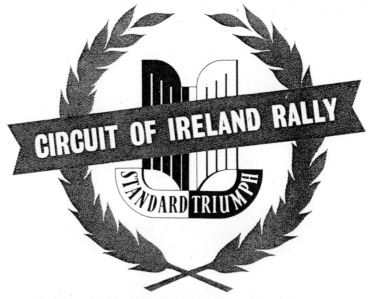

CIRCUIT OF IRELAND RALLY

STANDARD TRIUMPH

TRIUMPH T.R.3
SWEEPS THE BOARD

1ST OUTRIGHT WINNER	**2**ND	**3**RD
P. B. HOPKIRK J. SCOTT	J. D. TITTERINGTON B. McCALDIN	A. D. MALCOLM W. MULLEN
5TH	**6**TH	**7**TH
D. A. HENDERSON A. M. GAMBLE	J. CHESNEY J. CLARKE	R. C. McKINNEY F. D. ERSKINE

ALSO WINNER OF TEAM PRIZE

CLASS 4   GRAND TOURING CARS   **1**ST **2**ND **3**RD **4**TH **5**TH **6**TH

Subject to official confirmation

THIS IS THE THIRD SUCCESSIVE YEAR THAT TRIUMPH T.R.'S
HAVE WON THIS 1,500 MILE INTERNATIONAL RALLY

Another example of
STANDARD-TRIUMPH RELIABILITY

Triumph Motor Co. (1945) Ltd., Coventry, England. *A subsidiary of The Standard Motor Co. Ltd.*

Triumph TR 3

Triumph bask in competition glory in 1958, as the TR 3'A' sports continues to add to a growing reputation. The TR was a true sports car, rather than a poseur's tourer, and was popular in America as well as at home. This approach to enthusiasts is in marked contrast to the emphasis on luxury trimmings and decoration which pervaded much of the saloon car market. The "Circuit of Ireland Rally" was not the most famous of events, but would be familiar to the enthusiasts at whom the advertisement was aimed.

greetings from **STANDARD** | **TRIUMPH**

Triumph Herald

As the fifties ended, the first signs of the lighthearted advertising which would develop in the sixties became apparent. This attractive piece showed a car which was radically different from its Standard Ten predecessor, and which marked the ingress of the Triumph name into what had formerly been Standard territory. Like the Mayflower before it, the Herald would offer an individualist small car to buyers, and, before long a wooden dashboard was adopted. The Herald became well-known for its separate chassis, borne more of body supply problems than of any clinging to old-fashioned practice. The styling, by Michelotti of Italy, was much more attractive than some indigenous proposals.

It all started with one cylinder

1903—First Vauxhall Ever Offered for Sale
Single cylinder, 4″ x 4½″, horizontal stroke.
Tiller steering. No reverse

Startled citizens were still stroking their chins over the horseless carriage, and saying it would never replace the horse, when the first Vauxhall puttered on to the road. What a wildly daring departure for a respectable firm of marine engineers! And what a long way Vauxhalls have travelled in the fifty years since!

Before long Vauxhalls were beating all comers for reliability and speed. In 1908 a 20 hp Vauxhall won the 2,000 Mile RAC Trial coupled with the Scottish Reliability Trials. In 1911 four 16 hp world's records were broken. In 1912 a new 20 hp world's record of 97.15 mph over 50 miles was set up. In 1913 the fabulous 30/98 Vauxhall, *the sports car of sports cars* was introduced. In the 1914 war the Vauxhall 25 was the No 1 staff car. It took King George V as near the front line as a car could go.

Between the wars, Vauxhall set new conceptions of motoring value by marrying economy and performance. The Cadet, the " Light Six ", the 10 hp made motorists of pedestrians in tens of thousands.

Today Vauxhall lead the way with the new Wyvern and Velox, so big and handsome, so powerful, inexpensive and economical, that the designer of that first single-cylinder tiller-steered marvel might well gasp at the revolution he began.

1908—Reliability—45 Years Ago! In the RAC and Scottish Reliability Trials this 20 hp Vauxhall became the world's first car to complete 2,000 miles without one involuntary stop

1910—First 20 hp Car to Beat 100 mph
was this Vauxhall which flashed down the Brooklands flying half-mile at 100.08 mph

1920—The Fabulous Vauxhall 30/98—" One of the greatest British high performance cars of all time ", winner of innumerable trophies. And still winning today in vintage car events

Vauxhall Motors Limited
Luton, Beds.

And Today—The six cylinder, spacious, comfortable, reliable Vauxhall Velox, an 80 mph high performance car—which combines economy with luxury. Price £535, plus £224.0.10 P.T. The 4 cyl. Wyvern £495, plus £207.7.6 P.T.

Vauxhall Velox E-type

A Golden Jubilee is always a good occasion on which to parade one's illustrious ancestors, and here GM's British subsidiary reminds modern buyers of the heritage they adopt when they buy the new saloons. It is not surprising that the older vehicles all date from pre-General Motors days, and it is ironic that early postwar Vauxhalls did not, as a rule, last for very long. These Vauxhalls were larger, smoother, and marginally slower than the equivalent Fords. They deserve a place in history for sheer stylistic exuberance.

Vauxhall value...
greater than ever for 1956

NEW FEATURES...NEW STYLING...NEW COLOURS...

Take a good look at the good looks of the new Vauxhalls. The wide-view panoramic rear window and the slimmer windscreen pillars are new. New too are the glossier finishes — in a wider-than-ever range of single colours, plus, on the Cresta, distinctive duotones alternated to give a three-colour effect. (See illustration.)

Other 1956 features include new and better brakes, new door-locks and window-winding mechanism, nylon upholstery options on some models, and many touches of refinement.

With all these extra features, Vauxhall value is greater than ever. Room for six and all their luggage. Outstanding performance with good economy in the 6-cylinder Velox and Cresta. Outstanding economy with quite surprising performance in the 4-cylinder Wyvern. Four-figure engineering at three-figure prices — purchase tax included! See these brilliant new models at your local Vauxhall dealers.

Vauxhall Motors Ltd · Luton · Bedfordshire.

688

Vauxhall Cresta E-type

This advertisement for the fast and flashy Cresta of 1956 is unusual in its use of the cutaway diagram, a form normally confined to sales brochures. By comparison with rival products, the E-type was unfashionably tall and bulbous – characteristics which the colour scheme and chromium plate attempted to disguise. 1956 also marked the abandonment of the simple pulldown side windows and pushbutton interior door releases that had been much-remarked upon features of earlier editions. Alas, the ''glossier finishes'' did little to cure the Vauxhall rust syndrome, which by now was entering motoring folklore.

Gracing today's finest cars

<small>FOR MORE COMFORT, more confidence on any road, fine car owners choose Goodyear 3·T Nylon tyres. Designed and styled to match up to today's higher performance cars, they combine the 'triple toughness' of exclusive 3·T Nylon cord with the extra security of the Self-Adjusting Tread. They're the safest, strongest, most luxurious tyres ever built.</small>

◇ 3·T ◇ NYLON TYRES by

GOOD/YEAR

THE WORLD OVER MORE PEOPLE RIDE ON GOODYEAR TYRES THAN ON ANY OTHER MAKE

Vauxhall Cresta PA

Unlike the Victor, the Cresta was generally considered handsome, even by those not naturally drawn to transatlantic styling. Of British cars, it was the Cresta whose design was the most uncompromisingly American, and this purple/lilac colour scheme is sober by comparison to some that were offered. The grille of this 1959 version gave those familiar with the 1956 Packard a feeling of dèja vu, but many features were unusual, such as the curve of the front quarterlight frame. The oval tail lamps would be echoed on the 1960 Mercury. This is a typical Goodyear advertisement of the period; the Ford Zodiac was another car portrayed in the series. Poses were invariably dramatic, lending interest to what is hardly the most exciting of components.

New low look
new low price★

the Series 2
Vauxhall Victor
Estate Car

Always acknowledged a very good looker, the new Series 2 Victor estate car is now better than ever. Here is new, straight-through, smooth-line styling . . . panoramic visibility, 4-door easy entrance, counter-balanced up 'n' down tail door, smoother roof line, sleeker front end styling and new wrap-around bumpers.

Take your choice of a wide range of attractive colours, dual or single . . . and take your loads in ease and *safety* in the 45 cubic feet all-usable loadspace. For this Series 2 Victor has honest-to-goodness estate car design, incorporating extra robust springs and rear axle, special axle ratio for more pulling power, larger section tyres . . . and many other outstanding ' designed-for-the-job ' features.

See the Series 2 Victors at your Vauxhall dealers now –
Victor Estate Car £605 plus £303.17s PT (£908.17s)
Victor Saloon £505 plus £253.17s PT (£758.17s)
Victor Super £530 plus £266.7s PT (£796.7s)
Victor de Luxe, Vauxhall's new luxury car, leather upholstery, etc. £565 plus £283.17s PT (£848.17s).

★ VICTOR SERIES 2 ESTATE CAR **£605** PLUS £303.17s PT TOTAL £908.17s.

Vauxhall Motors Limited · Luton · Beds.

Vauxhall Victor F-type Series II Estate Car

"Always acknowledged as a very good looker" was a risky opening to this advertisement, as the Victor was arguably the most controversially styled car of the period. This Series II looked less outrageous than the original, which became notorious for its propensity to rust. Even engines and rear springs could break loose on bad examples, while dangling headlamps and rotted bumpers were commonplace. Vauxhall advertisements of the period frequently concentrated on the car's utility, and, rusting apart, the car was good of its type. The "counter-balanced up 'n' over tail door" was an advanced feature for the time.

I thought, somehow, you'd have a Wolseley...

The Wolseley Owner mentions his car with a certain satisfaction for discrimination in such matters proclaims taste as well as judgment. Wolseley prestige, a legacy of fifty years of brilliant achievement, is reflected in the performance, luxury and distinction of the Six-Eighty and Four-Fortyfour, two outstanding cars in the English fine-car tradition.

The Wolseley Four-Fortyfour
4 cyl. 1,250 c.c. engine. Seating within wheelbase. Distinctive Gold-Medal winning coachwork. English leather upholstery. Controllable inbuilt ventilation system. Independent front suspension.

The Wolseley Six-Eighty
6 cyl. 2,214 c.c. engine. Exceptional Wolseley finish with polished walnut facia and window trim. Leather and Dunlopillo upholstery. Full 5-seater. Interior twin lights. Extra large luggage capacity.

Wolseley models are fitted with safety glass all round.

Buy wisely – buy

WOLSELEY

WOLSELEY MOTORS LTD., COWLEY, OXFORD.
London Showrooms : 12, Berkeley Street, W.1.
Overseas Business : Nuffield Exports Ltd., Oxford and 41, Piccadilly, London, W.1.

SERVICE IN EUROPE
Qualified Wolseley owners planning a Continental Tour are invited to see their Wolseley dealer for details of a free service to save foreign currency.

Wolseley 6/80 Saloon

It comes as a surprise to find a quintessentially 1980s advertising theme being used to promote, of all cars, a Wolseley, in the early fifties. The clothes and manners are of their period, but the setting and the message put the Wolseley in a proto-yuppie context which would remain largely unexploited by other manufacturers for many years. The upmarket effect is achieved not only by the clothes, conversation and, of course the car, but by the set of the individuals' faces. The Wolseley, it is implied, brings people together, which lends a particular humour to the slogan at the foot of the page. The painting of the car is not too accurate, however, and in this depiction the frontal aspect of the 6/80 is reminiscent of the pre-war Panhard Dynamic.

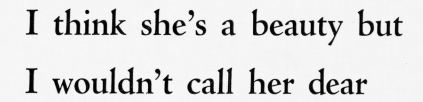

I think she's a beauty but
I wouldn't call her dear

THE WOLSELEY
FOUR-FORTYFOUR
There is also the Wolseley
Six-Eighty.

This smart and graceful car brings Wolseley ownership within the reach of the man who demands something better than a large-scale production model, without paying a high price. The forward positioning of its lively engine and a well balanced power-to-weight ratio—give the utmost comfort for both driver and passengers. Its road-holding and cornering capabilities are outstanding. Its many clever and sensible amenities belie its moderate price. It is a beautiful car you will be all the more pleased to own because of its remarkable value.

Buy wisely—buy

WOLSELEY

WOLSELEY MOTORS LTD., COWLEY, OXFORD
London Showrooms: 12, Berkeley Street, W.1. Overseas Business: Nuffield
Exports Ltd., Oxford and 41, Piccadilly, London, W.1.

Wolseley 4/44

A really awful pun introduces the smaller Wolseley, but if that makes the reader wince, the rest of the copy is more down to earth – verbose, but practical. The styling, appended grille apart, is arguably better balanced than that of the 6/90 which, with its straight-through flanks, is inclined from some angles to appear slabsided. The 4/44 outsold the 6/90 by a considerable margin. It shared much with the MG Magnette.

Gentlemen's Agreement

Giles and Charles have taken to being very civil about each other's Wolseley. "I must say," says Giles, "that your Four-Fortyfour has a wonderful performance for a 1¼ litre and is much more roomy and comfortable than one would suspect from its graceful lines." "And I'll admit," says Charles, "that I often hanker after the extra power and acceleration of your Six-Ninety. Let's agree anyhow that both cars have something which has always been characteristic of Wolseleys—a kind of quiet distinction—which is difficult to explain but which conveys a lot to one's friends."

WOLSELEY

Buy wisely—buy Wolseley

The Wolseley Six-Ninety. 2¼ litre. 6 cylinders. Seats six, giving each 18 ins. sitting width. Heater and screen washer. Foam rubber seats leather upholstered. Large unencumbered luggage boot. Superb performance and road holding. A no less distinguished Wolseley is the much sought after 1¼ litre Four-Fortyfour.

WOLSELEY MOTORS LIMITED . COWLEY OXFORD
London Showrooms: 12, Berkeley Street, W.1. Overseas Business: Nuffield Exports Ltd., Oxford and 41, Piccadilly, London. W.1.

Wolseley range, 1956

A tenacious pair are Charles and Giles, who are happy to stand around in the rain, talking across their wives with banale banter about their cars. It is amazing that they have any friends at all to whom the cars might convey anything, and it is ironic that this, one of a short sequence of advertisements, whose theme is so much of its own period, should introduce the "running story" concept in car advertising that has recently become popular.

COMPACT...
CONVENIENT...
...WOLSELEY

1500
FIFTEEN
HUNDRED

W197-C

TWELVE MONTHS'
WARRANTY
and backed by
BMC service

If you're the type of motorist (and you won't be alone) who is looking for livelier acceleration + out-of-the-ordinary comfort + easy-to-park dimensions ... then the Wolseley 1500 is the car for you. High power-to-weight ratio spells economy as well as sprightly performance. Words alone can't do justice to Wolseley luxury. Ask your dealer to arrange a demonstration and see for yourself. 1500 c.c. O.H.V. engine. 4-speed gearbox. 'Twin-top' performance in 3rd gear. Rack and pinion steering. Only 12 ft. 8 in. of car to park.

The Wolseley '1500' is available in two versions, Fleet Model and Family Model.
There is also the Wolseley 15/60 and the Wolseley 6/99.

WOLSELEY—A LUXURIOUS WAY OF MOTORING

WOLSELEY MOTORS LIMITED · COWLEY · OXFORD
London Showrooms: 12 Berkeley Street, W.1. Overseas Business: Nuffield Exports Ltd., Oxford and 41-46 Piccadilly, London W.1.

Wolseley 1500

In 1957 Wolseley re-entered a market which they had largely deserted since the war. The 1500 achieved success as a "luxury compact", even though it owed much to other BMC products. The body was derived from a proposed replacement for the Morris Minor, whose floorpan it shared. This advertisement is without the mannered contrivances of earlier years, but the older buyer is courted with mention of the "twin-top" gearbox, which was essentially a 1930s preoccupation. The "Fleet" model was a detrimmed version, and was not called "fleet" because it was faster!

LINE...
LUXURY...
...WOLSELEY 15-60

W196/c

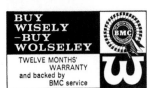
Here is a car to inspire pride of ownership. A car people admire for its clean, graceful lines and tasteful colour finishes. But only as a 15/60 owner can you fully appreciate the host of luxury features and delightful handling. Let your Wolseley dealer introduce you to the car which combines the excellence of Wolseley engineering and the brilliance of Pininfarina styling. 1½ litre O.H.V. engine. 4-speed gearbox. Central floor gear change. Panoramic vision. From £660 plus £276. 2. 6 P.T.

There is also the '1500' from £497 plus £208.4.2 P.T. and the 6/99 from £885 plus £369.17.6 P.T.

WOLSELEY—A LUXURIOUS WAY OF MOTORING

WOLSELEY MOTORS LIMITED · COWLEY · OXFORD

London Showrooms : 12 Berkeley Street, W.1.   Overseas Business : Nuffield Exports Ltd., Oxford and 41-46 Piccadilly, London, W.1

Wolseley 15/60

The new saloon was one of a generation of 1½-litre family cars with Pininfarina styling introduced in 1959. The reference to "delightful handling" should be read with some circumspection, as the considerable rear overhang and narrow track precluded anything sporting. Giles and Charles and their tortured vocabulary have mercifully been banished, and while the car is still seen as an object to be admired as much as driven, the column-change has gone, too. The "Farina" saloons were very rugged, and many survive in daily use, unrestored.